# Poet's
# Choice

# Also by Robert Hass

# POET'S CHOICE

## Poems for Everyday Life

Selected and Introduced by

## ROBERT HASS

THE ECCO PRESS

Copyright © 1998 by Robert Hass

THE ECCO PRESS
100 West Broad Street
Hopewell, New Jersey 08525

Published simultaneously in Canada by
Penguin Books Canada Ltd., Ontario
Printed in the United States of America

Library of Congress Cataloging-in-Publication Data

Hass, Robert.
Poet's choice / by Robert Hass.
p.    cm.
Includes bibliographical references and index.
ISBN 0-88001-566-7
1. Poetry—History and criticism. 2. Poetry—Collections. I. Title.
PN1016.H37   1998        9723792
809.1—dc21

Designed by Susanna Gilbert, The Typeworks
The text of this book is set in Poliphilus

9  8  7  6  5  4  3  2

FIRST EDITION 1998

# Contents

# A Note to Readers

This is a book of poems, a notebook of a poet's readings in poetry over a period of about two years, and an experiment. It is designed for readers, and it is therefore meant to be lived with, dipped into, left on a bedside table or on the table by the chair that you find your way to in the moments when you need to collect yourself, snatch a moment of repose, or hold in place the moment just after you've turned off the television set to listen to the silence and see what your life feels like. I hope it is a reader-friendly book. I've included a brief commentary on most of the poems, a word or two to tell you something about the author or what attracted me to the poem in the first place. There are easy poems here and difficult poems—though no easy poem, if it's interesting, is really easy and no difficult poem is that difficult—old ones and new ones, poems that you might want to read once a year and poems that you can live with for weeks.

And that's it. That would be my entire introduction, but I need to say also that this book did not begin as a book. It is a gathering of newspaper columns. So there is another way to read it. You could almost say it has a plot.

It was conceived a couple of years ago over breakfast in a Washington hotel a few blocks from the offices of the *Washington Post* in the kind of room—rich, vaguely French, floral carpet, linen so white it produced even in that unlikely setting a sensation of rectitude, imitation American Victorian china with English tea-roses on it, and weak coffee served in old fluted sterling silver pots—where one imagines altogether different kinds of deals are usually conceived.

I had just begun my term as poet laureate of the United States, and

Nina King, the literary editor of the *Post,* had invited me to meet with her and two of the editors of the *Post*'s exceptionally literate Sunday supplement, *Book World,* Marie Arana-Ward and Michael Dirda. My agenda wasn't complicated: I wanted to get American poetry into the newspapers. And, as it turned out, the agenda of the *Post* editors wasn't very complicated either. They wanted to get poetry into newspapers.

I had rehearsed elaborate arguments for why poetry should appear in the pages of newspapers. I was going to start by saying that I thought poetry should be syndicated in this country like comics and advice columns, that newspaper readership in the United States was declining, especially among the young and that newspapers were responding by trying to be more like television—more color, more pictorials—when they ought to be trying to create what the newspapers of the nineteenth century set out to create, a nation of readers, that in their panic they had gotten it exactly wrong. A democracy, I wanted to say, meant that citizens could master and make judgements on complicated ideas. It meant a shared language that went a little further and deeper than TV and movie scripts. If "Read my lips" was the only line we had in common, how could we not have a debased public language? Etc.

My arguments turned out to be entirely unnecessary. Perhaps Nina King had also marshalled arguments to persuade me to select poems for the *Post.* If so, I didn't hear them. Nor do I remember exactly what we said, but *Poet's Choice* is what we arrived at. I had wanted a free hand to pick poems, old and new, mostly American poems, mostly contemporary, and a certain amount of poetry in translation. The editors at the *Post* received more books of new poems every year than they could review, so they had been thinking about having someone select poems from among the new books. And they were concerned that, if they started printing poems, they would be overwhelmed by the submission of new poems. But we both felt the same urgency about getting some of the liveliness and intensity of poetry into the world.

What we settled on was a weekly column. I had wanted simply to pick a poem a week. The editors thought it would be more appealing if I wrote a little about it. I wanted to be sure that my picking a poem to be printed did not preclude the book being reviewed; it would be no favor to a poet to print a poem and lose the poet the possibility of more extended attention. They agreed, of course. So the formula would be that three out of every four columns would include poems from new books. We would not print work that had not appeared in book form, so we would not be dealing with hundreds of poems to which we couldn't give a fair reading. Every fourth column I would have room to range. We weren't sure, in truth, if once a week was too much, both from the point of view of reader interest and of my schedule. Poets laureate spend lots of time in public. I knew I was going to be more busy than I had ever been in my life, and busy in new and demanding ways. But reading a column is a habit and we thought it had to appear at least that often if readers were going to come to expect it. So, by the time the table was cleared— the menu full of health-conscious items for Senate staffers and young reporters fresh from the gym: egg white omelets with melon slices, non-fat muffins with the texture of sand castles—we had a plan.

I emerged into the October sunlight very excited. I imagined people all over America reading a poem at Sunday breakfast, Robert Frost on the New England fall, Anna Akhmatova writing about waiting in line outside a Leningrad prison for political prisoners in 1922 to deliver warm socks to her son, a Slovene futurist, an African-American Beat from Newark, some young neo-punk poet breaking language to get the way the sun rises over the morally compromised landscape of West Hollywood. I imagined people cutting them out, putting them on the refrigerator under ladybug magnets, quoting them to each other at work. And I also began to feel an incipient sense of panic. I had committed myself to reading a book of poems a week, probably two or three. And to not missing a deadline. I have never been wonderful about deadlines.

So this book may be read as an anthology—I hope it will be read as an anthology—but it can also be read as the history of an experiment. I learned some things right away. For example, I came to realize that I was limited to poems of a more or less uniform length. If newspapers were going to run the column, they needed to know how long it was. I wanted, for example, to print William Carlos Williams's "Burning the Christmas Greens." I envisioned Americans, when they were burning the Christmas greens, calling to mind a poem by one of our great poets, a family doctor who wrote in the middle of the Second World War of watching the sudden, fierce flaming up of the pine needles and seeing the destruction of cities as he mused on the creative and destructive power of fire. It is what I think is meant by a culture, to live in a place where the memory of common acts and the power of language give us a history. But "Burning the Christmas Greens" is about two pages long. So I dove back into my books looking for something else.

But I found that I did want, at least some of the time, to tie the poems I chose to the time of year, to a shared, reflective sense of the turning seasons. There is a poem about autumn by the Japanese poet Bashō:

> Deep autumn—
> my neighbor,
> how does he live, I wonder?

I wanted the poems to be, in part, about what our neighbors were thinking and feeling in the turning wheel of the year. This meant, in practice, that I was reading books of poetry in an altogether new, and not always desirable, way: rifling them, in moments stolen from travel and public events, for poems of the season that were something under forty lines long. As soon as I realized what I was doing, I tried to correct it: the point was to find interesting poems, and to convey something of the variety of experience in our poetry.

And I found that the column quickly became a collaboration. Readers were not only very generous about writing to say they liked the column, they were full of questions and suggestions. They wrote to ask if I could identify lines that had been rattling around in their heads for years. Some wrote to ask if I would print a particular poem that puzzled them and comment on it. One woman, in Washington, Greek by birth, told me that I had to print a poem by the great poet Odysseus Elytis. I made a note to myself to dig out my copy of his poems, bought when he won the Nobel Prize, I think. But I was slow getting to it. At readings at the Library of Congress, panel discussions at the Holocaust Museum, gatherings of schoolchildren at the Smithsonian, she would come up to me afterward, raise one finger and whisper, "Elytis." In this way, to my

unexpected pleasure, the column also became a dialogue with my read-
ers, and as the column started getting picked up in syndication—it now
appears regularly or occasionally in about 35 newspapers—I began to
get these suggestions from all over the country.

My other collaborator was Marie Arana-Ward at the *Post*. Marie is,
as I already knew, a brilliant reviewer, and she became my editor and
first reader as well. I'd fax her a column from a hotel in Rochester or
Santa Fe, sometimes with two different poems because I couldn't decide
between them, usually with queries: Does this sound too lame or too
pedantic? Is this poem sentimental? Impenetrable? I would hear from
readers if it were either. I got thunderous denunciations from time to
time: How could you print that piece of garbage? Poems to which a yel-
low marker had been applied indicating which lines or phrases the
reader thought unoriginal; reasoned, often convincing arguments about
why I had completely missed the point of a poem. Marie not only re-
minds me when a deadline looms; she is a wonderfully shrewd and re-
sponsive reader. And this is the place to thank her.

So you may read this book at random, as an anthology, meant to feed
the part of us that poetry speaks to and that life seems so often to conspire
against. Or you can read it as a poet's notes on his reading. Or you can
read it as an experiment in journalism, a modest attempt, however im-
modestly conceived, to give us back what we are losing—a shared, liter-
ate public culture.

# WINTER

# Starting From Capitol Hill

So, I was sitting in my new office in the attic of the Jefferson Library, watching the October sun through a handsome open window glisten on the Capitol dome and wondering what a poet laureate could usefully do.

> It is difficult
> to get the news from poems
>     yet men die miserably every day
>     for lack
> of what is found there—

William Carlos Williams wrote. These are lines that poets know, and on this particular morning, I remembered that Williams had spent his professional life practicing family medicine in Rutherford, N.J. His lines are a prescription. What I needed to do was apply Dr. Williams's dose to the body politic. In a form, of course—this is a free country—in which people could take it or leave it.

Poetry appeared in newspapers almost as soon as the newspapers themselves appeared in the young American republic. There are famous instances. Our national anthem saw the dawn light as a poem entitled "The Defence of Fort McHenry," published in the *Baltimore American* in September of 1814, and Clement Moore, a professor of Hebrew at the Columbia Theological Union wandered from his scholarly chores to publish "A Visit from St. Nicholas"—the one American poem, I've read, that almost everyone can recite a little of—in the *Troy Sentinel* on the night before Christmas in 1823. Abraham Lincoln first saw print as a poet in a newspaper, and the few poems Emily Dickinson published in her lifetime appeared in the *Springfield Register,* touched up by the editor for popular consumption, and Henry David Thoreau wrote aphoristic couplets for a country paper. Toward the end of the century another widely loved American poem, Ernest Lawrence Thayer's "Casey at the Bat," was printed in the new paper of his college classmate William Randolph Hearst, the *San Francisco Examiner.*

This chorus of voices—"so many uttering tongues," Walt Whitman wrote—gave a shared language to American readers all through the 19th century. And in Whitman himself, a newspaperman from his teens, there is expressed an attitude toward reading and toward poetry that it's hard even to recover imaginatively in the last years of the 20th century. From "Song of Myself":

> Have you reckoned a thousand acres much? Have you reckoned
>    the earth much?
> Have you practiced so long to learn to read?
> Have you felt so proud to get at the meaning of poems?

I suppose what's so moving about this to me is what it tells us about 19th-century Americans: they were learning to read. Literacy is now such common currency, so much assumed as a human skill—at least until the recent grumpiness and stinginess of taxpayers has begun to reverse the process—that we forget how our great-grandparents struggled to attain it. And the kind of value their effort gave to the written word.

At the beginning of the 19th century not very many people could even sign their own names, perhaps 40 percent of the English and 25 percent of the French. The United States was already one of the most literate countries in the world, especially in New England where almost 90 percent of white males and something like 44 percent of white females could at least produce a signature. But the rates in Virginia and Pennsylvania were much lower, and outside these centers, on the farms and the frontiers, literacy was a luxury. And, of course, most African-Americans, almost a third of the population, could not read and were likely to get in serious trouble if they tried to teach themselves. From the early 1800s on, newspapers drummed for public education and for literacy. By the 1840s the common school movement took hold. A whole country was teaching itself to spell, and to sound out words, and to scratch them on slates and on paper and in ledgers. We have lost our sense of the heroic scale of this achievement. If we had it in memory, we would not be, so casually, letting it erode, as we seem to be doing in this decade. By the end of the 19th century, even as the country assimilated floods of immigrants, the reformers had succeeded. Public schools had been estab-lished, newspapers flourished, and most people, black and white, men and women, could read.

And they read poems, and children memorized them, and recited them aloud in the classroom. Not necessarily great poems. Perhaps the best-remembered piece of 1899 was Gellett Burgess's "The Purple Cow," which most readers can probably recite whether they want to or not. But poems nevertheless. Though it is counterintuitive to think so, more people and a greater percentage of the population read and write poetry now than did then. There is in fact a kind of boom under way in American poetry. Lots of books are being published, and they sell enough in small but steady numbers to earn their way. Almost every night in every city and college town in America there are poetry read-ings in bookstores and university halls and coffeehouses. And this phe-nomenon has even passed into the high schools. I've gotten letters in my office at the Library of Congress from students in Florida, Ohio, and Virginia telling me about their noontime poetry cafés.

Despite all this activity and interest, it is a fixed American belief that poetry does not fare as well in the United States as it does elsewhere. Elsewhere being almost everyone's favorite place. We have the definite idea that somewhere else—Greece, Chile, the Republic of Korea—everyone reads poetry and the words of national poets are on every cab-driver's lips. And it isn't true. Foreign writers, visiting the United States, always express surprise at the variety and intensity of the poetry readings and poetry scenes in American cities and towns. What we do not have any longer is the tradition of poetry in our daily newspapers.

For whatever reasons, almost as soon as widespread literacy was achieved in the United States, poetry got lost as a common possession. So I had the idea that what this country needed was Dr. Williams's dose: a good five-cent poem, or a poem in every pot, or a poem to read lips with. And the editors at *Book World* have graciously offered to supply the spoon. Or the match. Or the stockpot. Whatever. ("Whatever" is the current sit-com writer's idea of a funny line. It's meant to call up young professionals a little too stressed to sweat the details. And poetry, like any art, thrives on attention to detail. It teaches the pleasure of attention to detail.) And so, in these pages, for a while, we are going to offer you a poem a week. Meant for your pleasure. Meant to begin to reclaim, from the artists among us working with language at its most intense and exact, the power and resonance that come from a speech held in common.

I will be picking the poems, mostly from new books but also from what belongs already to our common inheritance. One week it might be a shrewd, blues-tinged lyric like the ones Langston Hughes published in the 1920s in Harlem's *Amsterdam Record*. There's one, for example, called "Evil":

> Seems like what drive me crazy
> Don't have no effect on you,
> So I'm going to keep on at it,
> Till it drives you crazy, too.

Or one of Thoreau's couplets from the *Concord Journal*:

> The wind that blows
> Is all that anybody knows.

Or something from the European avant-garde like this little koan-like piece from the Slovenian poet Tomas Salamun, in the translation of Charles Simic:

> Emptiness! my bride!
> Who whistles? who listens?

But a handsome place to start might be with one of our grand old poets. Last week came the announcement that Stanley Kunitz of New York City and Provincetown, Mass., had, in his 90th year, received the National Book Award in poetry for a gathering of his recent work, *Passing Through: The Later Poems* (Norton). Though the announcement did not say so, I am pretty certain it is the first time in our history that the award went to an artist in his tenth decade. He was born in Worcester, Mass., in 1905, a life in poetry that spans the century, and one of the plea-

sures of his late work—as if he had been taking Dr. Williams's advice—
is its undiminished aliveness. There is news in poems. And, for me at
least, the news in this one has to do with listening to an old man, awake
at night beside his wife of many years and still shaken by the erotic drama
of what must be—the poem is a little ambiguous on this score—his
dreams. Here's the poem:

THE ABDUCTION

Some things I do not profess
to understand, perhaps
not wanting to, including
whatever it was they did
with you or you with them
that timeless summer
when you stumbled out of the wood,
distracted, with your white blouse torn
and a bloodstain on your skirt.
"Do you believe?" you asked.
Between us, through the years,
from bits, from broken clues,
we pieced enough together
to make the story real:
how you encountered on the path
a pair of sleek, grey hounds,
trailed by a dumbshow retinue
in leather shrouds; and how
you were led, through leafy ways,
into the presence of a royal stag,
flaming in his chestnut coat,
who kneeled on a swale of moss
before you; and how you were borne
aloft in triumph through the green,
stretched on his rack of budding horn,
till suddenly you found yourself alone
in a trampled clearing.

That was a long time ago,
almost another age, but even now,
when I hold you in my arms,
I wonder where you are.
Sometimes I wake to hear
the engines of the night thrumming
outside the east bay window
on the lawn spreading to the rose garden.
You lie beside me in elegant repose,
a hint of transport hovering on your lips,
indifferent to the harsh green flares
that swivel through the room,
searchlights controlled by unseen hands.
Out there is childhood country,
bleached faces peering in
with coal for eyes.
Our lives are spinning out
from world to world;
the shapes of things
are shifting in the wind.
What do we know
beyond the rapture and the dread?

I think this was written when he was 80.

I will be back next week, attending to the season as we enter the December dark. And did I say, you should read these poems out loud? Everybody loves the idea of that older eloquence. Here's your chance to start.

---

Decenber. The wind is getting raw, and I sometimes think of Seamus Heaney's plain lines—

Alders dripping, birches
Inheriting the last light,
The ash tree cold to look at.

Trees of a northern climate, of course. Heaney, who received the Nobel Prize for Literature this week in a ceremony in Stockholm, was born a Catholic near Belfast. In the middle of the 1970s, when the violence in Northern Ireland began to intensify, he withdrew to county Wicklow in the Republic of Ireland and wrote the poems that make up *North,* the book of his that gave a steady, canny, uncompromising moral focus to the tribal violence that had erupted among his neighbors. The poem I was remembering is the last one in that book. A comet appears (and fails to appear) in the poem; it seems to stand for the great comet of a poem that Heaney feels he should write, and it is also subtly connected, I think, to the idea of some heroic political stance. Violence is often bred out of he-roic stances. A troubled poem, half guilty, half defiant, beautifully made, it stakes out a space for sanity in a violent place. And a December wind blows through it.

### EXPOSURE

It is December in Wicklow:
Alders dripping, birches
Inheriting the last light,
The ash tree cold to look at.

A comet that was lost
Should be visible at sunset.
Those million tons of light,
Like a glimmer of haws and rose-hips.

And I sometimes see a falling star.
If I could come on meteorite!
Instead I walk through damp leaves.
Husks, the spent flukes of autumn.

Imagining a hero
On some muddy compound.
His gift like a slingstone
Whirled for the desperate.

How did I end up like this?
I often think of my friends'
Beautiful prismatic counselling
And the anvil brains of some who hate me

As I sit weighing and weighing
My responsible *tristia*.
For what? For the ear? For the people?
For what is said behind-backs?

Rain come down through the alders,
Its low conducive voices
Mutter about let-downs and erosions
And yet each drop recalls

The diamond absolutes.
I am neither internee nor informer;
An inner emigre, grown long-haired
And thoughtful; a wood-kerne

Escaped from the massacre
Taking protective colouring
From bole and bark, feeling
Every wind that blows;

Who, blowing up these sparks
For their meagre heat, have missed
The once-in-a-lifetime portent,
The comet's pulsing rose.


A wood-kerne? Heaney is a poet who sends you to the dictionary.

Several weeks ago I found myself participating in a Sunday afternoon symposium on the subject of Poetry and Resistance at the U.S. Holocaust Museum, on the day after the assassination of Yitzhak Rabin. One of those lucid and sunny fall days—so clear it felt that one ought to have something clear to say about that tragedy, about violence, about the making and unmaking of the world. Then, days later, I came across a new book by Susan Stewart, who lives in Philadelphia. It's called *The Forest*. The poems deal with many of the ghosts in the forests of the 20th century. It's not an easy book, brutal, mournful, intellectually demanding, but beautifully written. One part of the book, "Cinder," begins with this fierce small poem, which bears no title:

> We needed fire to make
> the tongs and tongs to hold
> us from the flame; we needed
> ash to clean the cloth
> and cloth to clean the ash's
> stain; we needed stars
> to find our way, to make
> the light that blurred the stars;
> we needed death to mark
> an end, an end that time
> in time would mend.
> Born in love, the consequence—
> born of love, the need.
> Tell me, ravaged singer,
> how the cinder bears the seed.

---

May Sarton died this year at the age of 80, just after a book of her poems, called *Coming Into Eighty*, was published. She spent most of her last years living by herself in a house by the sea in Maine and writing the poems and journals of her solitude that have attracted so many readers. Here is a poem from that book. It struck me that the poem echoes, intentionally or not, the most famous of all Christmas poems. Not a vision of St. Nick on this December night, and maybe more interesting for that.

DECEMBER MOON

Before going to bed
After a fall of snow
I look out on the field
Shining there in the moonlight
So calm, untouched and white
Snow silence fills my head
After I leave the window.

Hours later near dawn
When I look down again
The whole landscape has changed
The perfect surface gone
Criss-crossed and written on
Where the wild creatures ranged
While the moon rose and shone.

Why did my dog not bark?
Why did I hear no sound
There on the snow-locked ground
In the tumultuous dark?

How much can come, how much can go
When the December moon is bright,
What worlds of play we'll never know
Sleeping away the cold white night
After a fall of snow.

Perhaps the best-known New Year's poem in English Thomas Hardy's "The Darkling Thrush." I often think about it because the bird in the poem is so wonderfully described, completely beat up, singing its improbable song in the bleak English winter. The poem was written, in Hardy's peculiarly old-fashioned style, at the end of the first year of the 20th century, and what was to come gives the poem an even darker flavor. It is newly available in *The Essential Hardy* (Ecco), edited by Nobel Laureate Joseph Brodsky, who also contributes a brilliant essay on Hardy. Here is the poem:

### THE DARKLING THRUSH

I leant upon a coppice gate
    When Frost was spectre-gray,
And winter's dregs made desolate
    The weakening eye of day.
The tangled bine-stems scored the sky
    Like strings of broken lyres,
And all mankind that haunted nigh
    Had sought their household fires.

The land's sharp features seemed to be
    The Century's corpse outleant,
His crypt the cloudy canopy.
    The wind his death-lament.
The ancient pulse of germ and birth
    Was shrunken hard and dry,
And every spirit upon earth
    Seemed savorless as I.

At once a voice arose among
    The bleak twigs overhead
In a full-hearted evensong
    Of joy illimited;
An aged thrush, frail, gaunt, and small,
    In blast-beruffled plume,

Had chosen thus to fling his soul
  Upon the growing gloom.

So little cause for carolings
  Of such ecstatic sound
Was written on terrestrial things
  Afar or nigh around,
That I could think there trembled through
  His happy good-night air
Some blessed Hope, whereof he knew
  And I was unaware.

---

Something new for the New Year. Quietly, for the last decade, Gertrude Stein has been making a comeback. The world knows her for saying that a rose is a rose is a rose is a rose, and for saying of Oakland, Calif., that there's no there there. But the young have been discovering the sexual puns in pieces like "Tender Buttons" and "Lifting Belly," very daring in 1910, and this generation's avant-garde has been attracted by her experiments with breaking the rules of grammar that make our agreed-upon picture of the world. She found our agreed-upon picture of the world boring and suspect. A rose is a rose is a rose is a rose. One of the most interesting of the small presses, Sun & Moon, has just published an anthology that commemorates this interest, *The Gertrude Stein Awards in Innovative American Poetry, 1993–1994*, edited by Douglas Messerli.

Here from that book are a couple of pieces by a young New York City poet named Laynie Brown:

MEMORY IS THE VESSEL A SHELL BECOMES

The darkness was not at all transparent, so that turning to look behind me even the small path dissolved except for what appeared to be a punctuated flashing of solitary eyes. Peripheral vision test. Not meeting a single step or light in passing. This small patch of night is an accomplice, a relative to the larger galaxies. How easily we forget our history, with such certainty. Into the past as a mirror, into the self as a meteor.

## IN ORDER TO FIND YOUR ABSOLUTE CALENDAR

Listen more often to things. A necessary movement for achiev-ing stillness, looking back listening to the bottom, recognizing these things as skills. They were sad not seeing themselves as ade-quate machines. The burning dish invites a presence; a place shared by coincidence rather than by regularity. A room filled with madness. Not madness but the red called divine. Move on account of water. This rose is the same as a week. Dark ash pre-cedes crystal. An unmistakable murmur.

---

Forrest Hamer is a psychologist, African-American, born in Goldsboro, N.C., who grew up in the years of the free-dom marches and the desegregation of schools in the South. He went to Yale and teaches now at the University of California at Berkeley. And he has just published a first book of poems that remem-bers that Southern town and the feeling of those years. One of the things poetry can do is put you in possession of other people's experience. The famous formulation of this fact was made by the Chinese poet Li Po who wrote to his friend, the other of the great T'ang dynasty poets, Tu Fu: "Thank you for letting me read your new poems. It was like being alive twice." Here is a piece by Forrest Hamer from his *Call and Response,* published by Alice James Books/University of Maine at Farmington.

### LESSON

It was 1963 or 4, summer,
and my father was driving our family
from Ft. Hood to North Carolina in our 56 Buick.
We'd been hearing about Klan attacks, and we knew

Mississippi to be more dangerous than usual.
Dark lay hanging from trees the way moss did,
and when it moaned light against the windows
that night, my father pulled off the road to sleep.

Noises
that usually woke me from rest afraid of monsters
kept my father awake that night, too,
and I lay in the quiet noticing him listen, learning
that he might not be able always to protect us

from everything and the creatures besides,
perhaps not even from the fury suddenly loud
through my body about this trip from Texas
to settle us home before he would go away

to a place no place in the world
he named Viet Nam. A boy needs a father
with him, I kept thinking, fixed against noise
from the dark.

---

Here's a poem for everyone who caught this winter's feast of Jane Austen films, or sat through last season's PBS serial version of *Middlemarch*. It's from a new book, *An Early Afterlife* (Norton), by Linda Pastan. It takes a surprising turn at the end, as the work of this clear-eyed and nourishing poet often does:

THE ENGLISH NOVEL

In the English Novel, where I spent my girlhood,
I used to think chilblains were a kind of biscuit,
and everything was always pearled with fog—

the moors with their purpling heather
and the beveled windows where the heroines,
my sisters, waited for heroes
who would find them eventually, after one or both
threaded their way through some kind of moral
labyrinth, shadowed and thorny. He was worth waiting for,
and anyway the slowness of the clocks was deliberate
as if minutes, like pence, had different meanings then.
There was no polyester. Everything was brocade and velvet,
even the landscapes, those hills embroidered
with flowers, though sex was hardly mentioned
it was clearly a scent in the air like the sachets
in cupboards, subtle but pervasive as the smell
of lavender or viburnum or tallow from all the smoky,
snuffed-out candles. Furniture and forests, marriages
were eternal then, and though there was always a plot
it hardly mattered. As for too much coincidence,
doesn't the moon always wander through the sky at the exact
moment the lovers are wandering through the park, even today,
even in this city with its fake Victorian facades?
And all the familiar faces we notice at the movies
Or across a restaurant, couldn't they be our half-brothers
or cousins, lost once in the deep and mysterious gene pool—
descendants, some of them, of Emma and Mr. Knightley,
or the ones with Russian faces descended from Ladislaw maybe,
who could have come from a place just a few hours by carriage
from the shtetl where my great-great-grandmother
somehow acquired her blond hair and blue blue eyes?

---

One of the pleasures of going into my office at the Library of Congress is opening the letters in which citizens make use of their great national resource—"a grand literary storehouse," Mark Twain called it—by asking the poet laureate to help identify lines of poetry that have been rattling around in their heads. One writer wanted to know what poem and what poet these lines came from:

> Home is the sailor, home from the sea,
> And the hunter is home from the hill.

Another had lines in mind that he thought perhaps came from a poem called "The Mower" and that was perhaps from medieval English. Here is how he remembered the lines:

> For Juliana comes, and she,
> What I do to the grass, does to my love and me.

Another woman remembered, apropos of the spirit of this session of Congress, some lines her grandfather used to recite about a golf course near a mill in New England where the working children could watch the golfers on the other side of the fence. She thought the last line went like this:

> The laboring children can look out
> And see grown men at play.

Finally another writer asked from what poem came William Butler Yeats's line about "the foul rag-and-bone shop of the heart." This one I'll answer here. The line is from the last stanza of "The Circus Animals' Desertion," a poem that was published in *Last Poems*, after his death in January 1939. It's a poem in which he accuses himself of preferring art to life:

> Players and painted stage took all my love,
> And not those things that they were emblems of.

The circus animals of the title are all the images he conjured in his poems:

Those masterful images because complete
Grew in pure mind, but out of what began?
A mound of refuse or the sweepings of a street,
Old kettles, old bottles, and a broken can,
Old iron, old bones, old rags, that raving slut
Who keeps the till. Now that my ladder's gone,
I must lie down where all the ladders start,
In the foul rag-and-bone shop of the heart.

---

So Joseph Brodsky is dead. Probably his lines will be re-membered in Russia the way the lines of his great masters Anna Akhmatova and Osip Mandelstam are. They were, as he was, ferocious refusers. Among us he will certainly be re-membered, because, when he was not much more than a boy, he stood up to the whole apparatus of the Soviet state—not, it would seem, out of some deeply formulated conviction, but because he hated stupid slogans and he viscerally hated being told what to do. His great passion was lit-erature, and he loved cities. His writing is immensely civilized, restless, chronically skeptical. These lines come to mind, thinking about his death. They're from Anthony Hecht's translation of Brodsky's "Lul-laby of Cape Cod":

Therefore, sleep well. Sweet dreams. Knit up that sleeve.
Sleep as those only do who have gone pee-pee.
Countries get snared in maps; never shake free
of their net of latitudes. Don't ask who's there
if you think the door is creaking. Never believe
the person who might reply and claim he's there.

This is the poem in which, not long after he had begun his exile in America, he wrote these lines:

I write from an Empire whose enormous flanks
extend beneath the sea. Having sampled two
oceans as well as continents, I feel that I know
what the globe itself must feel: there's nowhere to go.
Elsewhere is nothing more than a far-flung strew of stars,
    burning away.

I think it was because he grew up with the relentless din of propaganda that he did not believe in much. But he believed passionately in the word, and it was our gift that in his essays and poems, his teaching and his talk, we got to share it. The best of his Russian poems, translated into his own English, are sardonic and passionate at once. Like these lines from "A Part of Speech," which make a kind of epitaph:

    . . . and when "the future" is uttered, swarms of mice
    rush out of the Russian language and gnaw a piece
    of ripened memory which is twice
    as hole-ridden as real cheese.
    After all these years it hardly matters who
    or what stands in the corner, hidden by heavy drapes,
    and your mind resounds not with a seraphic "doh,"
    only their rustle. Life, that no one dares
    to appraise, like that gift horse's mouth,
    bares its teeth in a grin at each
    encounter. What gets left of a man amounts
    to a part. To his spoken part. To a part of speech.

One of my readers suggested, given the success of "The Postman," that I print a poem by the great Chilean Pablo Neruda, who figures in that film as a love poet. Which he was, among other things. So, for St. Valentine's day, here is a love poem by Pablo Neruda. It's in the translation of Stephen Mitchell. You can try, like the postman in the movie, writing it out in your own hand, sending it to your lover, and watching what happens. But maybe you'd better see the movie first.

SONNET XVII

I don't love you as if you were the salt-rose, topaz
or arrow of carnations that propagate fire;
I love you as certain dark things are loved,
secretly, between the shadow and the soul.

I love you as the plant that doesn't bloom and carries
hidden within itself the light of those flowers,
and thanks to your love, darkly in my body
lives the dense fragrance that rises from the earth.

I love you without knowing how, or when, or from where,
I love you simply, without problems or pride:
I love you in this way because I don't know any other way
    of loving
but this, in which there is no I or you,
so intimate that your hand upon my chest is my hand,
so intimate that when I fall asleep it is your eyes that close.

This translation can be found, along with others, in a book I edited with the translator, *Into the Garden: A Wedding Anthology*, published by HarperCollins. Neruda is an immense poet, on the order of Walt Whitman. Not reading him would be like going through life without ever having listened to Beethoven. But he's also uneven.

Stephen Mitchell and I argued about this poem. I simply didn't believe the line Neruda gives his speaker—whether that's meant to be Neruda himself or some imagined person like the postman in the movie: "I love you in this way because I don't know any other way of loving." I said, "Look, we all know more crazy and selfish ways of loving." And Stephen said, plausibly, "Well, the person in this poem loves with a completely open heart." And a woman friend, listening, said, "Oh yes, it's called co-dependency." I leave the debate to you.

My favorite volumes of Neruda translations are *Selected Poems*, edited by Nathaniel Tarn (Delta) and *Neruda & Vallejo*, edited by Robert Bly (Beacon).

---

The candidates for the National Book Critics Circle Award in poetry were announced recently. Five books were nominated, and we will have a chance to look at one poem from each in the next few weeks.

The most unusual of them is Ellen Bryant Voigt's *Kyrie*. Voigt is a Virginian by birth and has lived for many years in rural Vermont. She's long been admired by other poets for her rich, tough-minded, nourishing poems. "Passionate arguments against fate," one critic called them. *Kyrie* is a book mostly of sonnets, spoken by many different characters, that calls up an almost forgotten event, a harrowing epidemic of influenza that burned through the United States in the years 1918–19 and killed half a million people. The book begins with one family, country people, Bible readers, during the years of World War I, and branches out to speak in the voices of many victims and many bereaved. It calls up another America, in some ways more, in some ways less innocent than ours.

Voigt never tells us explicitly what drew her to this subject, but a small prologue poem ends with these lines:

> And who can tell us where there was an orchard,
> where a swing, where the smokehouse stood?

Perhaps the book asks us to see the AIDS epidemic through another lens, which was, of course, my first thought, but perhaps all epidemics are also metaphors for our fate and poets simply the stubborn keepers of memory. Here's one of the poems:

This is the double bed where she'd been born,
bed of her mother's marriage and decline,
bed her sisters also ripened in,
bed that drew her husband to her side,
bed of her one child lost and five delivered,
bed indifferent to the many bodies,
bed around which all of them were gathered,
watery shapes in the shadows of the room,
and the bed frail abroad the violent ocean,
the frightened beasts so clumsy and pathetic,
heaving their wet breath against her neck,
she threw off the pile of quilts—white face like a moon—
*and then entered straightway into heaven.*

---

Another of the nominees for the National Book Critics Circle Award in poetry is James Merrill's *A Scattering of Salts.* Merrill, one of the most admired poets of his generation, died last year at the age of 68. So graceful he was and so elegant that one critic said he was to poetry what Fred Astaire had been to dance. Here's an uncharacteristic but perhaps timely poem. It's about snow and politics, and begins with a description of some other season's candidates:

SNOW JOBS

X had the funds, the friends, the plan.
Y's frank grin was—our common fate?
Or just a flash in just a pan?
Z, from the tender age of eight,
Had thirsted to officiate.
We hardly felt them disappear,
The crooked and the somewhat straight.
Now where's the slush of yesteryear?
Where's Teapot Dome? Where's the Iran

Contra Affair? Where's Watergate—
Liddy—Magruder—Ehrlichman?
Their shoes squeaked down the Halls of State,
Whole networks groaned beneath their weight,
Till spinster Clotho darted near
To shroud in white a running mate.
Ah, where's the slush of yesteryear?

Like blizzards on a screen the scan-
dals thickened at a fearful rate,
Followed by laughter from a can
And hot air from the candidate.
With so much open to debate,
Language that went in one ear
Came out the—hush! be delicate:
Where is the slush of yesteryear?

Omniscient Host, throughout your great
Late shows the crystal wits cohere,
The flaky banks accumulate—
But where's the slush of yesteryear?

It took me awhile to figure out the last stanza. God as the ultimate
late-show host, calling down the comedian of snow to cleanse the earth?
Something like that. And the spinster is, of course, not a political spin-
ster, but one of the Greek crones who spin out and cut the thread of life.

*A Scattering of Salts* was published by Alfred Knopf, which also
published the book many feel is Merrill's masterwork, a strange beauti-
ful long poem—a sort of cosmic comedy—about summoning spirits
through the medium of a Ouija board. It's called *The Changing Light at
Sandover.*

One of the many books by William Matthews, another of the National Book Critics Circle nominees in poetry, is called *Blues If You Want*. Matthews, a Midwesterner by birth, a professor of English at the City University of New York, sometimes takes his subjects from blues and jazz, and he himself writes with stylishness, with a bluesy elegance. *Time and Money* is the name of his new book, nominated as one of the best of 1995. Here's a poem, bristling, as his work does, with rue, irony, intelligence:

GRIEF

*E detto l'ho perche doler ti debbia*
   —*Inferno*, xxiv, 151

Snow coming in parallel to the street,
a cab spinning its tires (a rising whine
like a domestic argument, and then
the words get said that never get forgot),

slush and backed-up runoff waters at each
corner, clogged buses smelling of wet wool . . .
The acrid anger of the homeless swells
like wet rice. *This slop is where I live, bitch.*

a sogged panhandler shrieks to whom it may
concern. But none of us slows down for scorn;
there's someone's misery in all we earn.
But like a bur in a dog's coat his rage

has borrowed legs. We bring it home. It lives
like kin among the angers of the house,
and leaves the same sharp zinc taste in the mouth:
*And I have told you this to make you grieve.*

Elegance: Matthews quotes a line from one of the damned souls in Dante's Hell to get started and then translates it into plain English in the last line of his poem. Which saves him the trouble of saying explicitly what our cities have come to resemble. And subtlety: The undersides of the poem—the tires whining like a domestic argument, the evocation of the angers in a house—seem to be about other, more intimate hells. An-other elegance: Look at the rhymes; *rage* rhymes with *may* on the vowel sound, *wool* with *swells, bitch* with *each.* The pattern, for your inspection, is to rhyme the first and last line in each stanza, and also the two middle lines. He's a poet who listens to language. All this aside, what I admire about the poem is the lingering sense of some private grief that never even gets stated. It does stick in the mind like a bur.

---

The fourth of the books nominated for the National Book Critics Circle Award in poetry is *Cortege* (Gray-wolf Press) by Carl Phillips. Phillips is a younger poet, African-American, and that increasingly rare being, a classicist. He studied Latin and Greek at Harvard. His subject is eros. Here's a spare, unnerving example of his work, careful stanzas, the timing and phrasing immaculate:

FREEZE

The only light in the room,
moonlight, was
enough,

gave to his body on the bed
the suggestion of
stone drawn,

in relief, up from the stone
rest of itself,
what art

always wants, to pull somehow
a life from what
isn't. At

the window, the first snow had
begun, early. Watching
its shadow

pass, slow, down his back, in
the same way my hand
sometimes

does—that unnoticed, that
determined to, anyway,
do it—

I began thinking elsewhere, of
a life from before.
I wondered

if the snow fell there, too.

---

The last of the National Book Critics Circle nominees in poetry is Lynda Hull's *The Only World* (Harper Perennial). Hull, who struggled in her life with alcohol and drug addiction, died in 1994 in an automobile accident at the age of 39. This posthumous book includes an introduction by her husband, the poet David Wojahn, and an afterword by her poet friend Mark Doty. Painful poems, full of lyric intensity. All of them are too long to quote in full. Best, perhaps, to quote a few passages. A memory of her teenage years in Newark:

We perfected all the gestures,
　　JoAnn's liquid hands sculpting air,

her fingers' graceful cupping, wrist turning,
　　　　palm held flat, "Stop in the Name of Love,"
　　pressing against the sky's livid contrails,

a landscape flagged with laundry, tangled
　　　　aerials and billboards, the blackened
　　railway bridges and factories ruinous

in their fumes

There's a suite of poems for another friend named Emily, who gets
mixed up, in the sequence, with Emily Dickinson:

Out here the pavement's
a slick graffitied strip: *There's more to life
than violence.* Someone's added, *Yes, Sex and Drugs.*
Hello, Plague Angel. I just heard your wings
hiss off the letter on my table—Emily's
in prison again, her child's lost to the State,
Massachusetts. Fatigue, pneumonia,
the wasting away. In the secret hungering,
the emptiness when we were young would come
the drug's good sweep like nothing else,
godly almost the way we'd float immune
& couldn't nothing touch us, nothing.

Later in the sequence, she seems to write about what her poems were
looking for:

A prayer that asks

where in the hour's dark moil is mercy?

Ain't no ladders tumbling down from heaven
for what heaven we had we made. An embassy

of ashes & dust. Where was safety? Home?

# SPRING

Constantin Cavafy (1864–1933) is one of the great poets of the 20th century. He lived out his life writing poetry in Greek in an obscure district of Alexandria, Egypt, where he worked for the British administration of the city as a special clerk in the Irrigation Service of the Ministry of Public Works. From this small corner of the great world, in a life almost without event, he fashioned a myth out of his city and its history. These remarkable poems are well known to almost all poets, and they should be better known by American readers. They're available now in an elegant small edition, *The Essential Cavafy*, edited by one of the poet's best English translators, Edmund Keeley. Here is one of his most famous poems:

## WAITING FOR THE BARBARIANS

What are we waiting for, assembled in the forum?

  The barbarians are due here today.

Why isn't anything happening in the senate?
Why do the senators sit there without legislating?

  Because the barbarians are coming today.
  What laws can the senators make now?
  Once the barbarians are here, they'll do the legislating.

Why did our emperor get up so early,
and why is he sitting at the city's main gate
on his throne, in state, wearing the crown?

  Because the barbarians are coming today
  and the emperor is waiting to receive their leader.
  He has even prepared a scroll to give him,
  replete with titles, with imposing names.

Why have our two consuls and praetors come out today
wearing their embroidered, their scarlet togas?

Why have they put on bracelets with so many amethysts,
and rings sparkling with magnificent emeralds?
Why are they carrying elegant canes
beautifully worked in silver and gold?

Because the barbarians are coming today
and things like that dazzle the barbarians.

Why don't our distinguished orators come forward as usual
to make their speeches, say what they have to say?

Because the barbarians are coming today
and they're bored by rhetoric and public speaking.

Why this sudden restlessness, this confusion?
(How serious people's faces have become.)
Why are the streets and squares emptying so rapidly,
everyone going home so lost in thought?

Because night has fallen and the barbarians have not come.
And some who have just returned from the border say
there are no barbarians any longer.

And now, what's going to happen to us without barbarians?
They were, those people, a kind of solution.

---

In poems small things can count for a lot. Consider the
difference a comma makes in these two lines:

The woods are lovely, dark, and deep.
The woods are lovely, dark and deep.

To my ear this makes two entirely different—almost opposite—meanings. In the first line the emphasis is evenly distributed. Lovely=dark=deep. It's a peaceful, undisturbing scene. In the second "dark and deep" is the *kind* of loveliness, and the second phrase is spoken rapidly, as if it were a darting glance at a darkness and deepness one doesn't want to linger over too long.

The second line is the one Robert Frost wrote in one of the best known of all American poems, "Stopping by Woods on a Snowy Evening." The first line was written by a Dartmouth professor named Edward Lathem who edited Robert Frost's poems after his death and took it upon himself to correct Frost's punctuation. Lathem's version appeared in *The Poetry of Robert Frost* (Holt Rinehart Winston) in 1969 and has been the standard version available ever since. Poets have been complaining about this incredible rewriting of Frost's poems for 25 years. Now, at last, thanks to the Library of America, Frost's poems are available as he wrote them. Here is the rather scary poem Robert Frost actually wrote:

### STOPPING BY WOODS ON A SNOWY EVENING

Whose woods these are I think I know.
His house is in the village, though;
He will not see me stopping here
To watch his woods fill up with snow.

My little horse must think it queer
To stop without a farmhouse near
Between the woods and frozen lake
The darkest evening of the year.

He gives his harness bells a shake
To ask if there is some mistake.
The only other sound's the sweep
Of easy wind and downy flake.

The woods are lovely, dark and deep,
But I have promises to keep,
And miles to go before I sleep,
And miles to go before I sleep.

---

April marks the first annual celebration of National Poetry
Month. Publishers, bookstores, and community arts or-
ganizations all over the country will sponsor special
events this month to honor the presence of poetry in our culture. It's also
the beginning of spring. Here's my favorite American poem of this time
of year. Not T.S. Eliot's "April is the cruelest month" or Emily Dickin-
son's "A little Madness in the Spring / Is Wholesome Even for a King,"
but William Carlos Williams's "Spring and All," a poem on the sub-
ject by a man who made his living delivering babies:

SPRING AND ALL

By the road to the contagious hospital
under the surge of blue
mottled clouds driven from the
northeast—a cold wind. Beyond, the
waste of broad, muddy fields
brown with dried weeds, standing and fallen

patches of standing water
the scattering of tall trees

All along the road the reddish
purplish, forked, upstanding, twiggy
stuff of bushes and small trees
with dead, brown leaves under them
leafless vines—

Lifeless in appearance
dazed spring approaches—

They enter the new world naked
cold, uncertain of all
save that they enter. All about them
the cold, familiar wind—

Now the grass, tomorrow
the stiff curl of wildcarrot leaf

One by one objects are defined—
It quickens: clarity, outline of leaf

But now the stark dignity of
entrance—Still, the profound change
has come upon them: rooted, they
grip down and begin to awaken

---

As part of National Poetry Month, the Library of Congress
will be hosting a celebration of the tradition of American
nature writing. Among the poets who will be present is
the Kentucky farmer, poet, novelist, and agrarian thinker Wendell
Berry. It's spring. Here's a farmer's poem of the long cycle of renewal:

THE CURRENT

Having once put his hand into the ground,
seeding there what he hopes will outlast him,
a man has made a marriage with his place,
and if he leaves it his flesh will ache to go back.

His hand has given up its birdlife in the air.
It has reached into the dark like a root
and begun to wake, quick and mortal, in timelessness,
a flickering sap coursing upward into his head
so that he sees the old tribespeople bend
in the sun, digging with sticks, the forest opening
to receive their hills of corn, squash, and beans,
their lodges and graves, and closing again.
He is made their descendant, what they left
in the earth rising into him like a seasonal juice.
And he sees the bearers of his own blood arriving,
the forest burrowing into the earth as they come,
their hands gathering the stones up into walls,
and relaxing, the stones crawling back into the ground
to lie still under the black wheels of machines.
The current flowing to him through the earth
flows past him, and he sees one descended from him,
a young man who has reached into the ground,
his hand held in the dark as by a hand.

This comes from *Collected Poems, 1957–82*. Readers may also want to get to know Berry's essays in *A Continuous Harmony* and *Another Turn of the Crank,* and his novels *A Place on Earth* and *The Memory of Old Jack.*

---

Perhaps our best-known nature poet and ecological thinker in this half-century is Gary Snyder. A volume of his essays, *A Place in Space,* appeared recently. Snyder is associated with the emergence of the Beat poets in San Francisco in the 1950s and became a legend to the young when he served as the model for Japhy Ryder, the central character in Jack Kerouac's popular novel *The Dharma Bums.* Snyder, a champion of the wild, is anything but a wild man. When the rowdy Beats were making a name for themselves in the

late '50s, he was in a monastery in Kyoto, Japan, receiving formal train-
ing in Zen Buddhism. Like Henry David Thoreau, whom he in some
way resembles, Snyder's work is characterized by an elegant, attentive,
disciplined mind and a poetry based in the rhythms of physical work.
Hard to represent the grandeur and complexity of his work, so I won't
try. Here's a sweet recent poem that gets the quality of his attention:

SURROUNDED BY WILD TURKEYS

Little calls as they pass
through dry forbs and grasses
Under blue oak and gray digger pine
In the warm afternoon of the forest-fire haze;

Twenty or more, long-legged birds
all alike.

So are we, in our soft calling,
passing on through.

Our young, which trail after,

Look just like us.

The best available collection of his work is *No Nature: New and Se-
lected Poems* (Pantheon). It contains the early Beat poems of his student
days, the poems of his work as a logger and Forest Service lookout in the
Northwest, the poems of Japan, temple-quiet, and his Buddhist train-
ing, the Pulitzer Prize-winning volume *Turtle Island,* some of his transla-
tions of classical Chinese poetry, and the later poems of family life and
creaturely life in the foothills of the Sierra Nevada. Including a piece
called "Some Good Things to Be Said for the Iron Age," which ends:

the taste
of rust

When I was appointed Poet Laureate, my first thought was that I was going to have to wear this honor in a way that stood for the whole tradition of West Coast writing. The great elder of that tradition is the poet Robinson Jeffers of Carmel, Calif., who wrote about the California coast from the early 1920s until his death in 1962. When Jeffers settled in the picturesque little town of Carmel, it was not much more than a village; he fashioned there his long-lined poems that imitated the movement of the sea. The town grew up around him and became, partly because of his fame, a popular tourist attraction. Here is a late poem of his that seems particularly appropriate this month as the Library of Congress celebrates the tradition of American nature writing:

CARMEL POINT

The extraordinary patience of things!
This beautiful place defaced with a crop of suburban houses—
How beautiful when we first beheld it,
Unbroken field of poppy and lupin walled with clean cliffs;
No intrusion but two or three horses pasturing,
Or a few milch cows rubbing their flanks on the outcrop
    rockheads—
Now the spoiler has come: does it care?
Not faintly. It has all time. It knows the people are a tide
That swells and in time will ebb, and all
Their works dissolve. Meanwhile the image of the pristine
    beauty
Lives in the very grain of the granite,
Safe as the endless ocean that climbs our cliff.—As for us:
We must uncenter our minds from ourselves:
We must unhumanize our views a little, and become confident
As the rock and ocean that we were made from.

## VIEW OF THE LIBRARY OF CONGRESS FROM
## PAUL LAURENCE DUNBAR HIGH SCHOOL

A white substitute teacher
At an all-black public high school,
He sought me out saying my poems
Showed promise, range, a gift,
And had I ever heard of T.S. Eliot?
*No.* Then Robert Hayden perhaps?

Hayden, a former colleague,
Had recently died, and the obituary
He handed me had already begun
Its journey home—from the printed page
Back to tree, gray becoming
Yellow, flower, dirt.

No river, we skipped rocks
On the horizon, above Ground Zero,
From the roof of the Gibson Plaza Apartments.
We'd aim, then shout the names
Of the museums, famous monuments,
And government buildings

Where our grandparents, parents,
Aunts, and uncles worked. Dangerous duds.
The bombs we dropped always fell short,
Missing their mark. No one, not even
Carlton Green who had lived in
As many neighborhoods as me,

Knew in which direction
To launch when I lifted Hayden's
Place of employment—
The Library of Congress—

From the obituary, now folded
In my back pocket, a creased map.

We went home, asked our mothers
But they didn't know. Richard's came
Close: Somewhere near Congress,
On Capitol Hill, take the 30 bus,
Get off before it reaches Anacostia,
Don't cross the bridge into Southeast.

The next day in school
I looked it up—The National Library
Of the United States in Washington, D.C.
Founded in 1800, open to all taxpayers
And citizens. *Snap!* My Aunt Doris
Works there, has for years.

Once, on her day off, she
Took me shopping and bought
The dress shoes of my choice.
Loafers. They were dark red,
Almost purple, bruised—the color
Of blood before oxygen reaches it.

I was beginning to think
Like a poet, so in my mind
Hayden's dying and my loafers
Were connected, but years apart,
As was Dunbar to other institutions—
Ones I could see, ones I could not.

This poem is by Thomas Sayers Ellis, a 33-year-old poet born and
raised in Washington, D.C. It's from a new anthology, *The Garden
Thrives: Twentieth Century African-American Poetry,* edited by Clarence
Major and published by HarperPerennial. More about this book next
week.

L ast week in this space I printed a poem by a young African-American poet from Washington, D.C., named Thomas Sayers Ellis. It's called "View of the Library of Congress from Paul Laurence Dunbar High School" and tells the story of a gifted high school student, growing up in Washington, who is introduced by a white substitute teacher who recognizes his talent to the work of the poet Robert Hayden, a former Consultant in Poetry at the Library of Congress. This high school student in the poem has never heard of Hayden or of the Library of Congress and then remembers that the library is where his favorite aunt works, the one who bought him a new pair of loafers, beautiful shoes "the color of blood before oxygen reaches it." It's a wonderfully subtle poem about, among other things, the distance between people and public institutions in Washington.

The poem comes from a remarkable new anthology, edited by the poet and novelist Clarence Major, of 20th-century African-American poetry—the first anthology to convey the sweep and achievement of African-American poets in this last troubled, inspiring and disheartening hundred years. The book, which begins with the early poets of the century—especially Paul Laurence Dunbar who died in 1906—conveys the rich explosion of the Harlem Renaissance, the commanding mid-century work of Gwendolyn Brooks and Robert Hayden, the poetry of the civil rights and black arts movement, of the current generation that includes Poet Laureate Rita Dove and Pulitzer Prize-winner Yusef Kommunyaka, and a surprising group of young poets including Ellis, who—to complete the circle—went to Paul Laurence Dunbar High School.

Many readers will already know it, but here is Dunbar's best-known poem, written as the century began, in the high tide of Jim Crow and the Ku Klux Klan. It's also, you'll notice, a poem of the North American spring:

SYMPATHY

I know what the caged bird feels, alas!
    When the sun is bright on the upland slopes;
When the wind stirs soft through the springing grass,
And when the river flows like a stream of glass;

When the first bird sings and the first bud opes,
And the faint perfume from its chalice steals—
I know what the caged bird feels!

I know why the caged bird beats his wing
    Till its blood is red on the cruel bars;
For he must fly back to his perch and cling
When he fain would be on the bough a-swing;
    And a pain still throbs in the old, old scars
And they pulse again with a keener sting—
I know why he beats his wing.

I know why the caged bird sings, ah me,
    When his wing is bruised and his bosom sore,
When he beats his bars and he would be free;
It is not a carol of joy or glee,
    But a prayer that he sends from his heart's core
But a plea, that upward to heaven he flings—
I know why the caged bird sings!

---

This year's Pulitzer Prize in poetry was awarded to Jorie Graham for her selected poems, *The Dream of the Unified Field* (Ecco Press). Graham, raised in Italy by expatriate American parents, was educated here and in Paris, and lives in Iowa City with her husband, the writer and poet James Galvin. A poet of luminous intelligence, she has been called a postmodernist, which in her case means, I think, that she can turn the simplest act of seeing into thralled, passionate quest. She can make you see how complicated, what a wonder, perception is. Here's a poem about seeing an updraft of fallen leaves from the rear-view mirror of her car.

## STEERING WHEEL

In the rear-view mirror I saw the veil of leaves
suctioned up by a change in current
and how they stayed up, for the allotted time,
in absolute fidelity to the force behind,
magenta, hovering, a thing that happens,
slowly upswirling above the driveway
I was preparing to back clear out of—
and three young pine trees at the end of that view
as if aghast with bristling stillness—
and the soft red updraft without hesitation
aswirl in their prickly enclosing midst—
and on the radio I bent to press on,
a section with rising strings plugging in,
crisp with distinctions, of the earlier order.
Oh but I haven't gotten it right.
You couldn't say that it was matter.
I couldn't say that it was sadness.
Then a hat from someone down the block
blown off, rolling—tossing—across the empty macadam,
an open mouth, with no face round it,
O and O and O and O—
"we have to regain the moral pleasure
of experiencing the distance between subject and object,"
—me now slowly backing up
the dusty driveway into the law
composed of updraft, downdraft, weight of these dried
                            mid-winter leaves,
light figured-in too, I'm sure, the weight of light,
and angle of vision, dust, gravity, solitude,
and the part of the law which is the world's waiting,
and the part of the law which is my waiting,
and then the part which is my impatience—now; *now?*—

though there are, there really are,
things in the world, you must believe me.

---

Jorie Graham, who received the Pulitzer Prize last month for her selected poems, *The Dream of the Unified Field,* also recently published an anthology, *Earth Took of Earth: 100 Great Poems of the English Language* (Ecco Press). I've had it as a bedside book for about a month.

It's wonderful to have a completely fresh reading of the canon of English and American poetry by a distinguished contemporary poet. Here, for the sheer pleasure of it, and to usher in summer, is the poem she chose to represent Robert Burns:

GREEN GROW THE RASHES

*Chorus*
Green grow the rashes, O;
　Green grow the rashes, O;
The sweetest hours that e'e I spend
　Are spent amang the lasses, O!

There's nought but care on ev'ry han';
　In ev'ry hour that passes, O;
What signifies the life o' man,
　An' 'twere not for the lasses, O.
　　　　　*(Chorus)*

The warly race may riches chase,
　An' riches still may fly them, O;
An' though at last they catch them fast,
　Their hearts can ne'er enjoy them, O.
　　　　　*(Chorus)*

But gie me a canny hour at e'en
  My arms about my dearie, O;
An' warly cares, an' warly men,
  May a' gae tapsalteerie, O!
          *(Chorus)*

For you sae douce, ye sneer at this,
  Ye're nought but senseless asses, O;
The wisest man the warl' saw,
  He dearly loved the lasses, O.
          *(Chorus)*

Auld nature swears, the lovely dears
  Her noblest work she classes, O.
Her prentice han' she tried on man,
  An' then she made the lasses, O.
          *(Chorus)*

    The format is one poem per poet. Graham likes intense language—rich poems—and it makes for a gorgeous book, full of surprises and a gift for summer reading.

    *Tapsalteerie,* by the way, is, according to the OED, a Scots version of *topsy-turvy,* a word whose origin is accorded a fairly long, very learned, and inconclusive treatment. *Tirve* is an obsolete noun, meaning "to turn, or overturn." *Topsy* is either "topside" or, possibly, "topsail." To complicate matters, *tapsail* was a name given to a kind of East Indian cotton. So the English *topsy-turvy* may have gotten into a sort of double-exposure pun on *tapsail* or *topseil* that combined "all askew" with an added Scots sneer at stupid London fashions. One of the lovely things about old poems is the old play in language they keep alive.

Louise Glück is a poet so widely admired that half of the review of her new book, *Meadowlands*, in the *New Yorker* was about the pre-publication gossip. Glück is an exquisite writer, and her typical form is the brief, resonant, haunted, tragic lyric. The buzz about *Meadowlands* (the husband in the book is a Giants fan) was that it was funny, "Glück laughs" being a sort of literary equivalent of "Garbo talks." Here's the first poem in the book, which unfolds almost like a novel, a contemporary marriage seen, with wry irony, through the lens of myth:

PENELOPE'S SONG

Little soul, little perpetually undressed one,
do now as I bid you, climb
the shelf-like branches of the spruce tree;
wait at the top, attentive, like
a sentry or look-out. He will be home soon;
it behooves you to be
generous. You have not been completely
perfect either; with your troublesome body
you have done things you shouldn't
discuss in poems. Therefore
call out to him over the open water, over the bright water
with your dark song, with your grasping,
unnatural song—passionate,
like Maria Callas. Who
wouldn't want you? Whose most demonic appetite
could you possibly fail to answer? Soon
he will return from wherever he goes in the meantime,
suntanned from his time away, wanting
his grilled chicken. Ah, you must greet him,
you must shake the boughs of the tree
to get his attention,
but carefully, carefully, lest
his beautiful face be marred
by too many falling needles.

This puts me in mind of a haiku by Bashō:

> Let my faithless lover
> crawl to me
> through the spiked quince hedge.

Delicious in Glück is the timing of the offbeat line breaks: "it behooves you to be / generous," "You have not been completely / perfect."

---

Who would have thought that Dante's *Inferno* would appear on American best-seller lists some 600 years after the fact? But it did, a couple of years ago, in a version by Robert Pinsky, which was instantly hailed as a classic of verse translations—"one hell of a poem," a witty reviewer said.

Now Pinsky's own opulent gifts are on display in *The Figured Wheel: New and Collected Poems, 1966–1996*, 30 years of work by one of our best poets. More on this book later, but here—a long way from the Tuscan hell of the 13th century—is a dreamy small poem for the summer to come:

SONNET

Afternoon sun on her back,
calm irregular slap
of water against a dock.

Thin pines clamber
over the hill's top—
nothing to remember,

only the same lake
that keeps making the same
sounds under her cheek

and flashing the same color.
No one to say her name,
no need, no one to praise her,

only the lake's voice—over
and over, to keep it before her.

---

Probably the best-known poem about fathers is Sylvia Plath's "Daddy." It is a little too long to print here, and it is not altogether friendly toward the male parent. I recommend that you look it up. It ends, to give you the flavor:

There's a stake in your fat black heart
And the villagers never liked you.
They are dancing and stamping on you.
They always *knew* it was you.
Daddy, daddy, you bastard, I'm through.

Another well-known poem is "My Papa's Waltz," by Theodore Roethke. Roethke was born in 1908 in upper Michigan, where his father had a greenhouse and a wholesale florist business. So this poem must remember evenings after work in about 1916:

MY PAPA'S WALTZ

The whiskey on your breath
Could make a small boy dizzy;
But I hung on like death:
Such dancing was not easy.

We romped until the pans
Slid from the kitchen shelf;
My mother's countenance
Could not unfrown itself.

The hand that held my wrist
Was battered on one knuckle;
At every step you missed
My right ear scraped a buckle.

You beat time on my head
With a palm caked hard with dirt,
Then waltzed me off to bed
Still clinging to your shirt.

A waltz rhythm, and a poem poised, as I read it, between love and
terror.

And then there is Robert Hayden's "Those Winter Sundays." Hay-
den was also born in Michigan, in Detroit, in 1913. He was adopted by
a couple in his neighborhood at the age of two when his mother had to
give him up. His adoptive father was a laborer and a stern Baptist.
Hayden went on to become the first African-American Consultant in
Poetry at the Library of Congress. Here is how he remembers his father:

THOSE WINTER SUNDAYS

Sundays too my father got up early
and put his clothes on in the blueblack cold,
then with cracked hands that ached
from labor in the weekday weather made
banked fires blaze. No one ever thanked him.

I'd wake and hear the cold splintering, breaking.
When the rooms were warm, he'd call,
and slowly I would rise and dress,
fearing the chronic angers of that house,

Speaking indifferently to him,
who had driven out the cold
and polished my good shoes as well.
What did I know, what did I know
of love's austere and lonely offices?

# SUMMER

L et's see. How about summer, postmodernism, and the Midwest. From an anthology of contemporary Iowa poets, a look at the heartland by Jane Miller.

SEPARATION

Well my Cadillac now that the hog herding has begun
        big ones spray-gunned
is this the permission we long for
        not in prose or stone but in action?
electric-prodded out of the pen backed into the bloody aisle
        pigs chew pigs' tails
whack the metal feeders charge the gate
        so it's beauty in the end we were after or serenity?
slapped on the rump shoved at the truck
        who shall not ever again find anchorage
never feared July never feared June
        every one with an inconsolable mother . . .

My ballast
        I've scratched a key along the side of a white Camaro
in hog heaven the place one finds
        community possible desirable
my legendary embankment
        I will never get over you
I cruise the high-pitched scream of the engine
        my tenderloin my tetracycline
I want only to illuminate a tiny thing in a coat
        woolen cap and rubber boots
marked by a spray of red paint
        just where our lovers die.

This is from *Voices on the Landscape: Contemporary Iowa Poetry,* edited by Michael Carey. Jane Miller's *Memory at these Speeds: New and Selected Poems* is from Copper Canyon Press. If you want to know how she thinks about poetry (you know something of what she thinks about hog slaughter, traffic deaths, logical progression, and lost love) there is her *Working Time: Essays on Poetry, Culture and Travel* (University of Michigan Press).

---

For the Fourth of July: Here's a poem by Abraham Lincoln, written when he was 37 years old. There is a longer version, but this one was widely printed in newspapers around the country after his assassination in 1865:

MEMORY

My childhood's home I see again,
    And sadden with the view;
And still, as memory crowds my brain,
    There's pleasure in it, too.

O memory! thou midway world,
    'Twixt earth and paradise,
Where things decayed and loved ones lost
    In dreamy shadows rise,

And, freed from all that's earthly, vile,
    Seem hallowed, pure and bright,
Like scenes in some enchanted isle
    All bathed in liquid light.

As dusky mountains please the eye
    When twilight chases day;
As bugle notes that, passing by,
    In distance die away;

As, leaving some grand waterfall,
    We, lingering, list its roar—

So memory will hallow all
   We've known but know no more.

Near twenty years have passed away
   Since here I bid farewell
To woods and fields, and scenes of play,
   And playmates loved so well.

Where many were, but few remain
   Of old familiar things,
But seeing them to mind again
   The lost and absent brings.

The friends I left that parting day
   How changed, as time has sped!
Young childhood grown, strong manhood gray;
   And half of all are dead.

I hear the loved survivors tell
   How naught from death could save,
Till every sound appears a knell
   And every spot a grave.

I range the fields with pensive tread
   And pace the hollow rooms,
And feel (companion of the dead)
   I'm living in the tombs.

The longer version can be found in John Hollander's *American Poetry: The Nineteenth Century* (2 volumes; Library of America, 1993).

A new book by Denise Levertov, one of our admired senior poets. It's called *Sands of the Well* and like much of her work reads partly like an artist's sketchbook. Here are a couple of examples:

IN SUMMER

When the light, late in the afternoon, pauses among
the highest branches of the highest trees,
they stir a little as if in pleasure. Light and a passing breeze
become one and the same, a caress. Then the lower branches,
leaves or needles in shadow, take up the lilt
of that response, their green with its hint of blue forming
what, if it were sound, could be called
a chord with the almost yellow of those
the sunlight tarries with.

THE TRACE

My friendships with one to two, yes, three
men for whom I felt
the wildest, most painful longing,
some fragrance of those times,
like a box where once
the leaves of the exotic herb were kept,
an herb of varied properties, useful and dangerous,
long since consumed.

Something especially pleasant in summer about reading this book, which doesn't show off, is rarely clever, just attends as plainly as it can to the pulse of a life.

It's starting to be midsummer. Japanese poetry is so alert to the seasons that I thought I'd look there for a batch of summer haiku. Here are some by Bashō. First a famous one about a visit to a historic battlefield:

> Summer grass—
> all that's left
> of warriors' dreams.

And others in other moods:

> As for the hibiscus
> by the roadside,
> my horse ate it.

> A bee
> staggers out
> of the peony.

How do you convey a sense of summer heat without mentioning the words?

> A fishy smell—
> perch guts
> in the water weeds.

And here are a couple by Issa, who attends to small creatures:

> Mosquito at my ear—
> does it think
> I'm deaf?

> Even with insects
> Some can sing,
> some can't.

And this, for the permissions of summer:

Napped half the day—
no one
punished me.

---

Civilizations have their great periods of lyric poetry, and one of the greatest was T'ang dynasty China (A.D. 712–760), which produced three or four of the most remarkable poets in world literature. The best-loved of these was Li Po, and a new volume of his work has just appeared, in a rendering by one of the best contemporary translators of classical Chinese poetry, David Hinton.

The legend of Li Po is that he was an ethereal creature, a wild man and a wanderer. He was born in Central Asia to a distinguished family but liked to claim that he was partly of Turkish or Afghani stock: an exotic. He spent many years during the tumultuous T'ang period alternating between the roles of Taoist recluse and poetic wanderer. It's part of his story that he is said to have died when, drunk in a boat, he fell into a river and drowned trying to embrace the moon.

Here are a couple of his poems, in Hinton's translation:

AT YUAN TAN-CH'IU'S MOUNTAIN HOME

By nature, my old friend on East Mountain
treasures the beauty of hills and valleys.

Spring now green, you lie in empty woods,
still sound asleep under a midday sun,

your robe growing lucid in pine winds,
rocky streams rinsing ear and heart clean.

No noise, no confusion—all I want is
this life pillowed high in emerald mist.

## SOUTH OF THE YANGTZE, THINKING OF SPRING

How many times will I see spring green
again, or yellow birds tireless in song?

The road home ends at the edge of heaven.
Here beyond the river, my old hair white,

my heart flown north to cloudy passes,
I'm shadow in moonlit southern mountains.

My life a blaze of spent abundance, my old
fields and gardens buried in weeds, where

am I going? It's year's end, and I'm here
chanting long farewells at heaven's gate.

---

A delicious first book of poems by Laura Fargas, who is a Washington, D.C. attorney specializing, according to her book jacket, "in occupational safety and health litigation." The poems specialize in radiant plainness. Here's one:

## AMONG OUR GREAT CEREMONIES

A serious love touches the universe,
the two and one of it contributing to the sum of what's real.
Not that planets or even hydrogen atoms
begin falling toward you, yet something intensifies
where you are. The different light

shed by double stars. No consensus why they form,
or how they'll dim or dazzle, perishing.

And here's another. Kuan Yin is the Chinese goddess of mercy.
She's usually pictured as a figure of great serenity:

KUAN YIN

Of the many buddhas I love best the girl
who will not leave the cycle of pain before anyone else.
It is not the captain declining to be saved
on the sinking ship, who may just want to ride his shame
out of sight. She is at the brink of never being hurt again
but pauses to say, *All of us. Every blade of grass.*
She chooses to live in the tumble of souls through time.
Perhaps she sees spring in every country,
talks quietly with farm women while helping to lay seed.
Our hearts are a storm she trembles at. I picture her
leaning on a tree or humming or joining a volleyball game
on Santa Monica beach. Her skin shines with sweat.
The others may not know how to notice what she does to them.
She is not a fish or a bee; it is not pity or thirst;
she could go, but here she is.

---

All spring, after the readings at the Library of Congress, a
handsome and determined woman would come up to me
and say one word: "Elytis." Odysseus Elytis was a
Greek poet, born in Crete in 1911. He is in many ways the most sensu-
ous and alive of Greek poets, and he received the Nobel Prize for Litera-
ture in 1979. I think she wanted me to print one of his poems. So here, for
high summer and for her persistence, is a well-known prose poem. It
was written in about 1939. Like most European poets of that time, Elytis
was influenced by French surrealism, but he gave it an intensely Greek

flavor. The poem may be about a woman, but I think it is what it says it is, a kind of hymn to the visible and the beautiful:

FAMOUS NIGHT

. . . by the terraces, near the musical complaint of your hand's curve. Near your transparent breasts, the uncovered forests full of violets and vegetables and open palms of moon, far as the sea, the sea you caress, the sea that takes and leaves me leaving in a thou-sand shells.

Visible and beautiful I taste your good moment! I say that you communicate so well with people you raise them to the di-mension of your heart so none again can worship what belongs to him, what stirs like a tear at the root of every grass, the crown of each reached branch. I say that you communicate so well with the spring of things that your fingers match their fate. Visible and beautiful by your side I am whole! I want boundless paths at the crossroads of birds and of fair people, the gathering of stars that will co-rule. And I want to touch something, even your smallest firefly unsuspiciously jumping in the field's mane, so I can write with certain fire that nothing is transient in the world since the moment we chose, this moment we want over and above the all-gold contrariety, over and above the calamity of death's frost, in the path of each wind with love sighting our heart, in the superb gooseflesh of the sky that day and night is kneaded by the good-ness of stars.

---

Sharon Olds writes fierce, often funny and painful poems about family life: her life as a child, as a wife, mother, lover, her parents, her parenting. She looks right at things and her descriptions of what she sees can be startling. Here's a poem from her new book, *The Wellspring* (Knopf).

## HER FIRST WEEK

She was so small I would scan the crib a half-second
to find her, face-down in a corner, limp
as something gently flung down, or fallen
from some sky an inch above the mattress. I would
tuck her arm along her side
and slowly turn her over. She would tumble
over part by part, like a load
of damp laundry, in the dryer, I'd slip
a hand in, under her neck,
slide the other under her back,
and evenly lift her up. Her little bottom
sat in my palm, her chest contained
the puckered, moire sacs, and her neck—
I was afraid of her neck, once I almost
thought I heard it quietly snap,
I looked at her and she swivelled her slate
eyes and looked at me. It was in
my care, the creature of her spine, like the first
chordate, as if the history
of the vertebrate had been placed in my hands.
Every time I checked, she was still
with us—someday there would be a human
race. I could not see it in her eyes,
but when I fed her, gathered her
like a loose bouquet to my side and offered
the breast, greyish-white, and struck with
miniscule scars like creeks in sunlight, I
felt she was serious, I believed she was willing to stay.

Eavan Boland, born in Dublin in 1944, is one of the best-known Irish poets of her generation. A midcareer gathering of her work, *An Origin Like Water: Collected Poems 1967–87*, has recently appeared.

She's written about the life of women in Ireland and about Irish politics, but here is a mood-piece that gets, I think, some of the precision and subtlety of her art:

NOCTURNE

After a friend has gone I like the feel of it:
The house at night. Everyone asleep.
The way it draws in like atmosphere or evening.

One-o-clock. A floral teapot and a raisin scone.
A tray waits to be taken down.
The landing light is off. The clock strikes.
    The cat

comes into his own, mysterious on the stairs,
a black ambivalence around the legs of
    button-back
chairs, an insinuation to be set beside

the red spoon and the salt-glazed cup,
the saucer with the thick spill of tea
which scalds off easily under the tap. Time

is a tick, a purr, a drop. The spider
on the dining-room window has fallen asleep
among complexities as I will once

the doors are bolted and the keys tested
and the switch turned up of the kitchen light
which made outside in the back garden

an electric room—a domestication
of closed daisies, an architecture
instant and improbable.

---

L ate summer: I find myself reading around in books of po-
ems in the late afternoon or early evening the way you find
yourself sometimes craving, vaguely, an unexpected phone
call. Something about change, I suppose, about the way you can't tell
fullness from emptiness in the August twilight.

Anyway, I've come across some pleasing poems this way. One of the
poets I've been reading is Octavio Paz, the great Mexican poet and es-
sayist who received the Nobel Prize for Literature in 1993. Here's a little
poem about an orange, in Eliot Weinberger's translation:

ORANGE

Little sun
silent on the table,
permanent noon.
It lacks something:
                    night.

This comes from *A Tree Within,* a gathering of his poems written be-
tween 1976 and 1987 and published by New Directions.

And here is a short poem from a young American poet, Timothy
Liu. Liu is Chinese-American, California-born. He grew up in the
Mormon Church, and he is gay. His second book, *Burnt Offerings,* is
written in very plain, clear lines, almost as if they were fragments from
the Greek anthology. His subjects are passionate love, lust, loneliness.
They have some desire to shock. They can be brutally explicit about
longing, stolen love, and they have a deep aftertaste of spiritual search-
ing—like the erotic poems in the classical anthologies. Here's one that
will give you a sense of his style:

SUNDAY

And when they sat down in the morning
to bowls of cold cereal, each in turn
would notice the blades of the ceiling fan
spinning at the bottom of their spoons,
small enough to swallow, yet no one
ever mentioned it, neither looking up
nor into each other's eyes for fear
of feeding the hunger that held them there.

---

For Labor Day a poem about work and its product from
Robert Pinsky's rich, recently published collected poems.
It's a meditation on a shirt. And it manages to gather to it-
self the memory of the infamous Triangle Shirt Factory fire of 1911, a
turning point in American labor history, and references to the 17th-cen-
tury English poet George Herbert (who also wrote meditations) and to
Hart Crane's *The Bridge,* and a word about the history of kilts. But there
is nothing tricky here. This is about shirts and work:

SHIRT

The back, the yoke, the yardage. Lapped seams.
The nearly invisible stitches along the collar
Turned in a sweatshop by Koreans or Malaysians

Gossiping over tea and noodles on their break
Or talking money or politics while one fitted
This armpiece with its overseam to the band

Of cuff I button at my wrist. The presser, the cutter,
The wringer, the mangle. The needle, the union,
The treadle, the bobbin. The code. The infamous blaze

At the Triangle Factory in nineteen eleven.
One hundred and forty six died in the flames
On the ninth floor, no hydrants, no fire escapes—

The witness in a building across the street
Who watched how a young man helped a girl to step
up to the windowsill, then held her out

Away from the masonry wall and let her drop.
And then another. As if he were helping them up
To enter a streetcar, and not eternity.

A third before he dropped her put her arms
Around his neck and kissed him. Then he held
Her into space, and dropped her. Almost at once

He stepped to the sill himself, his jacket flared
And fluttered up from his shirt as he came down,
Air filling up the legs of his gray trousers—

Like Hart Crane's Bedlamite, "shrill shirt ballooning."
Wonderful how the pattern matches perfectly
Across the placket and over the twin bar tacked

Corners of both pockets, like a strict rhyme
Or a major chord. Prints, plaids, checks,
Houndstooth, Tattersall, Madras. The clan tartans

Invented by mill owners inspired by the hoax of Ossian,
To control their savage Scottish workers, tamed
By a fabricated heraldry: MacGregor,

Bailey, MacMartin. The kilt, devised for workers
To wear among the dusty clattering looms.
Weavers, carders, spinners. The loader,

The docker, the navvy. The planter, the picker, the sorter
Sweating at her machine in a litter of cotton
As slaves in calico headrags sweated in fields:

George Herbert, your descendant is a Black
Lady in South Carolina, her name is Irma
And she inspected my shirt. Its color and fit

And feel and its clean smell have satisfied
Both her and me. We have culled its cost and quality
Down to the buttons of simulated bone,

The buttonholes, the sizing, the facing, the characters
Printed in black on neckband and tail. The shape,
The label, the labor, the color, the shade. The shirt.

---

The end of summer. Years ago, the critic Northrup Frye proposed that most literary forms arose from human rituals dealing with the cycle of the seasons. Comedy, he argued, arose from fertility rituals associated with spring, tragedy from scapegoat and expiation rituals to clear the spent fields from lingering bad luck and uneasy spirits after the fall harvest. He worked it out as a kind of circular calendar: romance forms—stories that embody our dreams and ideals, Camelots and dream worlds like the one in Star Wars—for the fullness of summer, and the stripped-bare bitterness of satire for midwinter.

It's a vision of literature, and the moods of human life, turning on the wheel of the seasons. In lyric poetry this is a matter of moods and themes. The end of summer and the early fall have both a wistfulness and a freshening as we turn from what Wallace Stevens called "the credences of summer" toward a gorgeous and haunting change. The poem, of all others, that seems to get this moment is by Emily Dickinson:

As imperceptibly as grief
The summer lapsed away—
Too imperceptible at last
To seem like Perfidy—
A Quietness distilled
As Twilight long begun,
Or Nature spending with herself
Sequestered Afternoon—
The Dusk drew earlier in—
The Morning foreign shone—
A courteous, yet harrowing Grace,
As Guest, that would be gone—
And thus, without a Wing
Or service of a Keel
Our Summer made her light escape
Into the Beautiful.

This text is from *The Complete Poems of Emily Dickinson,* edited by Thomas H. Johnson, published by Little, Brown.

---

Virginia Hamilton Adair, who published her first book of poems this year, is 83 years old and blind. The book, *Ants on the Melon* (Random House), has gotten a lot of at‑tention partly because of the remarkable circumstance of such a literary debut and partly because the poems are so alive and surprising. Adair was born in New York City in 1913. She went to Mount Holyoke and to Radcliffe, married, raised three children, wrote her poems, some of which were printed in magazines, taught English, traveled, gardened, lived a life. Recently, at the urging of her friend, the poet Robert Mezey, and with his help, they assembled this book of a lifetime.

It's hard to know which poem to represent her by. Here's one—in form, a villanelle—that conveys something of her skill. The central drama of her life seems to have been the sudden suicide of her husband, Douglas Adair, an eminent American historian, in 1968 after a marriage of 35 years. This is a poem about, I think, the sense of betrayal she felt, after that event, because she continued to write.

DARK LINES

My lines hold fast and do not break
with drawing life from the cold sea.
I do this for my hunger's sake.

And when I climb the cliff to wake
from hounds of the night pursuing me,
my lines hold fast and do not break.

Forget me, Love, and never shake
with grief at infidelity;
I do this for my hunger's sake.

In this and many a poem I make
to sound my dark identity,
my lines hold fast and do not break.

Strange food for thought—why man would take
his rest beneath a hanging-tree!
—I do this for my hunger's sake.

Forgive me, Life, the famished ache
to swing across eternity—
my lines hold fast and do not break—
I do this for my hunger's sake.

# FALL

## BLACKBERRY EATING

I love to go out in late September
among the fat, overripe, icy, blackberries
to eat blackberries for breakfast,
the stalks very prickly, a penalty
they earn for the black art
of blackberry-making; and as I stand among them
lifting the stalks to my mouth, the ripest berries
fall almost unbidden on the tongue,
as words sometimes do, certain peculiar words
like *strengths* or *squinched,*
many-lettered, one-syllabled lumps,
which I squeeze, squinch open, and splurge well
in the silent, startled, icy, black language
of blackberry-eating in late September.

I came across this poem by Galway Kinnell, like an old friend, in an unexpectedly interesting new anthology, *Poetry in Motion: 100 Poems from the Subways and Buses* (Norton). It's a gathering of some of the poems that have appeared on public transportation in New York City between 1992 and 1997. It contains everything from haiku to bits of a chorus from a Greek tragedy to classic and contemporary European and American poets. All of the pieces are short. It makes a wonderful bedside book and there is the added pleasure of imagining the ways they might have been read by weary late night riders of crosstown buses or by commuters in packed subway cars in the summer heat. Imagine looking up suddenly at Seamus Heaney's translation of the first three lines of Dante's *Inferno:*

> In the middle of the journey of our life
> I found myself astray in a dark wood
> where the straight road had been lost sight of.

Or this epigram by the English poet Thomas Gunn:

## JAMESIAN

Their relationship consisted
In discussing if it existed.

*Poetry in Motion* is a joint project of the Poetry Society of America
and New York City Transit. It's an ongoing collaboration. You'd al-
most think we lived in a civilized country.

---

The book I've been living with this last month is *Other-wise,* by Jane Kenyon, who died last year of leukemia at the age of 47. It includes a selection of poems from her four published books, plus 20 poems previously unpublished and an af-terword by her husband Donald Hall. They lived together, quietly, on a New Hampshire farm and wrote their poems. Their life seemed attrac-tive to other people, and Bill Moyers made a prize-winning documen-tary film about them called "A Life Together." When Donald Hall was diagnosed with cancer a few years ago, she nursed him through treat-ment, and when he recovered, her illness appeared and proved to be un-treatable.

Kenyon wrote in the plain style—something of Frost, though her poems are much more interior, and something of the Russian poet Anna Akhmatova, though Akhmatova had an imperious and dramatic qual-ity very different from Kenyon's reflective, almost workmanlike attention to daily life. She seems to have struggled all her life with depression and this, instead of making her poems seem dark and unhappy, gives them a luminous gravity. Here's one of the later poems, atypical because it looks out of New England at the larger world.

MOSAIC OF THE NATIVITY:
SERBIA, WINTER 1993

On the domed ceiling God
is thinking

I made them my joy,
and everything else I created
I made to bless them.
But see what they do!
I know their hearts
and arguments:

"We're descended from
Cain. Evil is nothing new,
so what does it matter now
if we shell the infirmary,
and the well where the fearful
and rash alike must
come for water?"

God thinks Mary into being.
Suspended at the apogee
of the golden dome,
she curls in a brown pod,
and inside her the mind
of Christ, cloaked in blood,
lodges and begins to grow.

When I read this poem, I was struck at first by her imagination of—
what do they call the birth of gods?—theogony, the coming into being of
the Christ of suffering. But what stayed in my mind was the phrase
about our common condition: "the well where the fearful and rash alike
must come for water." This is the way her poems work on me. Some
phrase or image that I almost don't notice on first reading settles in and
haunts.

I was thrilled and surprised this week to hear that Wislawa
Szymborska received the Nobel Prize for Literature. Sur-
prised because I did not think the committee would give it to

another living Polish poet—Czeslaw Milosz won the prize in 1980—
and thrilled because she is unquestionably one of the great living Euro-
pean poets. She's accessible and deeply human and a joy—though it is a
dark kind of joy—to read.

Szymborska—her name is pronounced Vee-swah-vah Shim-bor-
skah—was born in 1923 and has lived almost all her life in Krakow. She
is, like so many Eastern European writers, an ironist. She writes, espe-
cially in her later years, a plain, almost bony verse, and she can stand for
the survival and resilience of imagination, in this last half-century. Her
poems will tell you more than I can. Here are three:

### IN PRAISE OF SELF-DEPRECATION

The buzzard has nothing to fault himself with.
Scruples are alien to the black panther.
Piranhas do not doubt the rightness of their actions.
The rattlesnake approves of himself without reservations.

The self-critical jackal does not exist.
The locust, alligator, trichina, horsefly
live as they live and are glad of it.

The killer-whale's heart weighs one hundred kilos
but in other respects it is light.

There is nothing more animal-like
than a clear conscience
on the third planet of the Sun.

### RETURNS

He came home. Said nothing.
Though it was clear something unpleasant had happened.
He lay down in his suit.
Put his head under the blanket.
Drew up his knees. He's about forty, but not at this moment.

He exists—but only as in his mother's belly
seven layers deep, in protective darkness.
Tomorrow he will give a lecture on homeostasis
in megagalactic cosmonautics.
For now he's curled up, fallen asleep.

## PORTRAIT OF A WOMAN

She must be willing to please.
To change so that nothing should change.
It's easy, impossible, hard, worth trying.
Her eyes are if need be now deep blue, now gray,
dark, playful, filled for no reason with tears.
She sleeps with him like some chance acquaintance, like his one
    and only.
She will bear him four children, no children, one.
Naive yet giving the best advice.
Weak yet lifting the weightiest burdens.
Has no head on her shoulders but will have.
Reads Jaspers and ladies' magazines.
Doesn't know what this screw is for and will build a bridge.
Young, as usual young, as always still young.
Holds in her hands a sparrow with a broken wing,
her own money for a journey long and distant,
a meat-cleaver, poultice, and a shot of vodka.
Where is she running so, isn't she tired?
Not at all, just a bit, very much, doesn't matter.
Either she loves him or has made up her mind to.
For better, for worse, and for heaven's sake.

I've taken these poems from *Sounds, Feelings, Thoughts: Seventy Poems
by Wislawa Szymborska,* translated by Magnus Krynski and Robert
Maguire (Princeton University Press, 1981). Another translation is
*View with a Grain of Sand: Selected Poems,* translated by Clare Cavanagh
and Stanislaw Baranczak (Harcourt Brace, 1995).

She is a poet to live with. Asked once to comment on her art, she cited the words of Montaigne: "See how many ends this stick has!" It was, she said, "an unsurpassable model of the writer's craft and a constant encouragement to transcend the obvious with thought." And she is another such model.

---

Here, for the season and for the pleasure of it, is one of the most gorgeous poems in the English language. John Keats wrote it when he was 24 years old, after a walk in the cathedral town of Winchester. He died a year later, in Rome, of consumption.

TO AUTUMN

I

Season of mists and mellow fruitfulness,
   Close bosom-friend of the maturing sun;
Conspiring with him how to load and bless
   With fruit the vines that round the thatch-eves run;
To bend with apples the mossed cottage-trees,
   And fill all fruit with ripeness to the core;
     To swell the gourd, and plump the hazel shells
   With a sweet kernel; to set budding more,
And still more, later flowers for the bees,
Until they think warm days will never cease,
   For Summer has o'er-brimmed their clammy cells.

II

Who hath not seen thee oft amid thy store?
   Sometimes whoever seeks abroad may find
Thee sitting careless on a granary floor,
   Thy hair soft-lined by the winnowing wind;
Or on a half-reaped furrow sound asleep,

Drowsed with the fume of poppies, while thy hook
   Spares the next swath and all its twined flowers:
And sometimes like a gleaner thou dost keep
Steady thy laden head across a brook;
Or by a cider-press, with patient look,
   Thou watchest the last oozings hours by hours.

III

Where are the songs of Spring? Ay, where are they?
   Think not of them, thou hast thy music too,—
While barred clouds bloom the soft-dying day,
   And touch the stubble-plains with rosy hue;
Then in a wailful choir the small gnats mourn
   Among the river sallows, borne aloft
     Or sinking as the light wind lives or dies;
And full-grown lambs loud bleat from hilly bourn;
   Hedge-crickets sing; and now with treble soft
   The red-breast whistles from a garden-croft;
     And gathering swallows twitter in the skies.

---

One of the most indelible poems of the 20th century, Paul Celan's "Todesfugue" or "Deathfugue" is notoriously difficult to translate. And I've just come across an extraordinary translation of the poem in John Felstiner's *Paul Celan: Poet, Survivor, Jew* (Yale University Press). The book is at once a biography of Celan, a study of his poems, and an account of the author's struggle with translation. It takes readers, especially readers who don't know German, inside the poems in a way that couldn't happen without Felstiner's story of the difficulties of getting their force from one language into another. For reasons of space, I'll say something about Celan here and print the poem next week.

Paul Celan was a Jewish poet educated to revere the traditions of

German poetry. He lost his parents in the concentration camps of the Third Reich and barely survived them himself. He is such an important figure because he was one of the first German-language artists of the postwar period to face the question of how it was possible to continue to make art out of the German language after the horror of Dachau and Auschwitz. And he struggled with the task all his life—until, on April 20, 1970, at the age of 49, in Paris where he had been living, he took his life by jumping from a bridge into the Seine.

Celan was born in 1920 in Czernowitz in the eastern reaches of the Austrian Empire. The town and the district had just become part of Romania. Czernowitz was a polyglot city of Romanian, German, Ukranian, Swabian, and Yiddish speakers, and it is one of the bitter ironies of his life that his mother took care that he spoke a correct literary German, rather than Yiddish or the impure, provincial German of Czernowitz. By 1940 he was a promising schoolboy poet, skilled in his mother tongue. The Soviets marched into Czernowitz in June; a year later the Germans invaded, drove the Jews into a ghetto, and began deporting them by the tens of thousands. On a summer night in 1942, while he was visiting friends nearby, his parents were taken. His father died of typhus in a camp at Transnistria in the fall of that year and in the winter his mother, who was also ill, was found "unfit to work" and shot. Celan, in the meantime, had been arrested and pressed into a German "labor battalion" run by the Romanian army and escaped deportation when the Russian army pushed west in 1944 and retook Czernowitz. After some years of wandering he made a life in Paris as a teacher of German. And tried to come to terms with his life and his language.

In his last years his wrestling with the language grew spinier, more strange and hermetic. The poems are hard. They seem to be trying to break the language and reinvent it. And, hard as they are, they are also haunting. There is a very good book of recent translations of Celan's later work, *Breathturn,* by Pierre Joris, published by Sun & Moon Press. These brief, opaque poems will give you the flavor:

Paths in the shadow-break
of your hand.

From the four-finger-furrow
I root up the
petrified blessing

Whitegray of
shafted, steep
feeling.

Landinwards, hither
drifted sea-oats blow
sand patterns over
the smoke of wellchants.

An ear, severed, listens.

An eye, cut in strips,
does justice to all this.

---

Here is Paul Celan's "Deathfugue," in the translation of John Felstiner, perhaps the best-known poem of the Holocaust. One of the powerful things about the translation is the way in which the translator lets the poem lapse back into German. The effect is harrowing and it allows us to feel, in the final lines, the force of the poem's final word, which is a Hebrew name:

DEATHFUGUE

Black milk of daybreak we drink it at evening
we drink it at midday and morning we drink it at night
we drink and we drink
we shovel a grave in the air there you won't lie too cramped
A man lives in the house he plays with his vipers he writes
he writes when it grows dark to Deutschland your golden hair

Margareta
he writes it and steps out of doors and the stars are all sparkling
he whistles his hounds to come close
he whistles his Jews into rows has them shovel a grave in the
    ground
he commands us play up for the dance

Black milk of daybreak we drink you at night
we drink you at morning and midday we drink you at evening
we drink and we drink
A man lives in the house he plays with his vipers he writes
he writes when it grows dark to Deutschland your golden hair
    Margareta
Your ashen hair Shulamith we shovel a grave in the air there you
    won't lie too cramped

He shouts jab this earth deeper you lot there you others sing up
    and play
he grabs for the rod in his belt he swings it his eyes are so blue
jab your spades deeper you lot there you others play on for the
    dancing

Black milk of daybreak we drink you at night
we drink you at midday and morning we drink you at evening
we drink and we drink
a man lives in the house your goldenes Haar Margareta
your aschenes Haar Shulamith he plays with his vipers

He shouts play death more sweetly this Death is a master from
    Deutschland
he shouts scrape your strings darker you'll rise then as smoke to
    the sky
you'll have a grave then in the clouds there you won't lie too
    cramped

Black milk of daybreak we drink you at night
we drink you at midday Death is a master aus Deutschland
we drink you at morning and evening we drink and we drink
this Death is ein Meister aus Deutschland his eye it is blue
he shoots you with shot made of lead shoots you level and true
a man lives in the house your goldenes Haar Margarete
he looses his hounds on us grants us a grave in the air
he plays with his vipers and daydreams der Tod ist ein Meister
    aus Deutschland

dein goldenes Haar Margarete
dein aschenes Haar Sulamith

---

Halloween has come and gone. But here, not too late, is a poem of the season out of the Southwest, so it marks not our odd, candy-and-spooks version of All Hallow's Eve but the Mexican and Mexican-American Day of the Dead. Janice Gould is a young poet from California. She is of European and Koyangk'auwi Maidu ancestry and her new book, *Earthquake Weather*, was recently published in the University of Arizona Press's American Indian Literary Series. Gould lives in Santa Fe and has taught American Indian literature at the University of Santa Fe in Albuquerque.

### THE DAY OF THE DEAD

I wish it were like this:
*el día de los muertos* comes
and we fill our baskets with bread,
apples, chicken, and beer,
and go out to the graveyard.

We bring flowers with significant colors—
yellow, crimson, and gold—

the strong hungry colors of life,
full of saliva and blood.

We sit on the sandy mounds
and I play my accordion.
It groans like the gates of hell.
The flames of the votives
flicker in the wind.

My music makes everything sway,
all the visible and invisible—
friends, candles, ants, the wind.
Because for me life ripens,
and for now it's on my side
though it's true I am often afraid.

I wear my boots when I play the old squeeze-box,
and stomp hard rhythms
till the headstones dance on their graves.

---

Here is a poem that should catch your eye, and give you something to think about. Frank Bidart is a poet like no one else now writing. For one thing he's interested in the human condition at its most extreme and intense. For another he uses typography to tell readers how to read his poems. He's the only poet I know who tries in this way to work not just with rhythm, which all poets do, but with the pitch of the voice. He uses italics for a kind of whispering intensity and capital letters for emphasis and the slight rise in tone that usually accompanies it in speech. Here's an example. Well, it's not an example. It's a poem about the human heart:

*up or down from the infinite C E N T E R*
*B R I M M I N G at the winking rim of time*

*the voice in my head said*

LOVE IS THE DISTANCE
BETWEEN YOU AND WHAT YOU LOVE

WHAT YOU LOVE IS YOUR FATE

❧

*Then I saw the parade of my loves*

*those PERFORMERS comics actors singers*

*forgetful of my very self so often I*
*desired to die to myself to live in them*

*then my PARENTS my FRIENDS   the drained*
*SPECTRES once filled with my baffled infatuations*

*love and guilt and fury and*
*sweetness for whom*

*nail spirit yearning to the earth*

❧

*then the voice in my head said*

WHETHER YOU LOVE WHAT YOU LOVE

OR LIVE IN DIVIDED CEASELESS

# REVOLT AGAINST IT

# WHAT YOU LOVE IS YOUR FATE

---

S tephen Dobyns began his writing career as a poice reporter
in Detroit. He is the author of nine books of poems and a
popular series of detective novels—of the hard-boiled Ray-
mond Chandler school—set in Saratoga Springs, N.Y. What kind of
poems come from a poet who is also a detective novelist? Dobyns's don't
aim at grace. They seem to distrust it, go on momentum, sometimes on
fury; they're attentive to the dark. Here's a poem from his most recent
book, *Common Carnage*.

### FLEAMARKET

A display of padlocks on a blanket on the sidewalk,
arranged as neatly as newborns in a hospital nursery—

I have known these souls, the ones who encourage
with a doorknob and frustrate with a key, who work

not to build something, but block something, the ones
who deny not from doubt or change of heart, but power,

the imposition of one muscle over another, men
and women who excite only to reject, that editor

who asked to read a friend's work, that teacher who
liked to tell students they were dumb, that shouter

who tried to shut down all other talk. A door
closes, a lock clicks, the division of space into

my space and other. Even in its shape, a padlock
duplicates the letters of the negative: the diagonal

imposed upon the zero. How hateful to be clustered
on a crowded blanket when each covets a single

blanket of its own. If you exist, then how can my
existence be of value? A locked room, a locked

soul, alone one can imagine one is anything:
a single multi-thorned rose, a window looking out

on the ocean, the embrace of the body by the body,
the eye that surveys the dark and sees only itself.

---

The most popular American Thanksgiving poem of the
19th century was written for children: "The New En-
gland Boy's Song About Thanksgiving Day." The au-
thor was Lydia Maria Child, one of those New England women writers
of the 19th century who seemed to turn their hand to everything. She
founded the first American children's magazine, was the author of *The
Frugal Wife,* numerous antislavery tracts, a history of the condition of
women, and several novels. The poem was published in Boston in 1844.
It begins:

Over the river and through the wood,
To grandfather's house we go;
The horse knows the way,
To carry the sleigh,
Through the white and drifted snow.

Contemporary poems of the season are mostly less idyllic, but they are also about family, about the way that the holiday asks families to come together—which sometimes means setting aside old troubles and which we are not always able to do. That's the subject of this poem by E.J. Miller Laino, from her book *Girl Hurt,* published last year by Alice James Books.

### RIVER BIRCH IN NOVEMBER

A branch hangs over the chain link fence,
leans to the left. Small leaves, all of them yellow,
look like premature Christmas lights and yesterday
the sky was gray-white over the ocean, the color
   it gets
when a storm is coming, but no rain came.
The sky stayed the color of my mother's kitchen curtains.
I didn't like it without the blue and yet,
as with all things I don't like, it got my attention
and I suppose, my respect.

I invited my brother to Thanksgiving dinner
but he wouldn't come unless I said I was wrong.
I couldn't do it. I had to hang up the telephone.

The ocean is gray the way I imagine
prison bars, a gray that says you can't get out.
There is no sky except gray sky. Only an airplane
could get above it. Within minutes
there would be clouds as white as the snow that sticks
to trees. If I could make clouds stick to me,
I'd fly today. Instead, I'm driving up Shore Road,
heading to a therapy session. A small section of ocean
says green. Begs green. A slight hint of it rises
up slowly. By the time I drive over the bridge,
the sea is steel again. Maximum security.

The winner of this year's National Book Award in poetry is Hayden Carruth's *Scrambled Eggs & Whiskey: Poems 1991–1995*, published by Copper Canyon Press. A much honored poet, Carruth received the National Book Critics Circle Award in 1992 for his last book, *Collected Shorter Poems, 1946–1991*, a volume that gathered together and summed up 45 years of work in poetry. A longtime New Englander, he is now 75 years old. He's always been a craftsman and *Scrambled Eggs & Whiskey* combines that assured craft with gruffness, ferocity, and something like domestic tenderness. The poems sit at the edge of old age; they look back, take stock, lash out, then return, often gratefully, to the present moment. "Snowstorm" is an instance:

SNOWSTORM

Everywhere men speak in whispers.
Tumult, many new ghosts. Storm
hurls itself across the valley
and careens from the ridges, swirls
of snow lapsing, leaping, colliding.
Outside on the highway a car
has rolled over the guard-rail,
two pickups have stopped, men
stand hunched with their hands
in their pockets. We are looking
from our kitchen windows, we
have called the country sheriff
and the wrecker, we have asked
the men to come in for coffee.
But they have said no, somewhat
sullenly. Earlier we had been speaking
of war in the Persian Gulf, of
all the wars and how armies are
everywhere now, hardly one
peaceful corner remaining
in the world. In strange cities

and in wastelands, on mountains
and on islands, young men and women
in clumsy uniforms and in unease
stand hunched with their hands
in their pockets, or drink
as much beer as they can, or screw
themselves silly—but mostly
they stand hunched with their hands
in their pockets, scornful of the native
people. Now through the snow
the men on the highway are vague
distant figures in a veiled world,
the car's lights are dim and unclear.
In our eaves and around our dormers
the wind cries and moans with increased
force, and the night comes on.

---

# A Brief Essay on Children's Poetry

I find myself browsing in the children's section of bookstores these days thinking about poetry and Christmas; think-ing—I have recently become a grandfather—about how to build a child's collection of poetry. That begins, of course, with Mother Goose. Why these magical poems continue to bewitch us is hard to know. There's a recent book by a French psychoanalyst and philosopher Nicholas Abraham which argues that rhythm belongs to the unsocial-ized body, that "living experienced, ungraspable rhythm . . . opposes conceptual thought with unrelenting mystery." That would explain why adults like the poems; but very young children, who are unsocial-ized bodies—well, scarcely socialized bodies—must love them because they marry living rhythm to magical order:

How many miles to Babylon?
Threescore miles and ten.
Can I get there by candlelight?
Yes, and back again.

It's the "back again" that must be reassuring to children. Though Mother Goose is also a realist. I used to love to look at my children's faces as they were being told that "all the king's horses and all the king's men / couldn't put Humpty together again." I think I looked at first to see if they were alarmed, but the look the kids had was often grave and satis-fied. It reminded me that one of my friends said her child's first word was "uh-oh," not, she said, as an expression of concern, but as a statement of fact.

Wildness, inevitability, and the music of language at its most skip-ping and dancing and orderly: It was Wallace Stevens who said that a good poem must just successfully resist the intelligence. And Mother Goose over and over again accomplishes that miracle. Parents may want to hunt up *The Oxford Annotated Mother Goose* in the library, to learn, for example, that "Georgie Porgie, pudding and pie" who kissed the girls and made them cry, came into the world in Jane Austen's time as a broadside jingle aimed at the Prince Regent. But for children the world of the nursery rhyme doesn't require explanation:

Hey diddle diddle, the cat and the fiddle.
The cow jumped over the moon.
The little dog laughed to see such sport,
And the dish ran away with the spoon.

One recent collection of these poems changes the third line, substi-tuting "fun" for "sport," as if children might be confused by the changed meaning of the word. But I think part of the pleasure of the poems is that they are also a kind of archaeology of the language. They may not lead us back, as the African-American rhyme does in Toni Morrison's *The Song of Solomon,* to the secret of origins, but it seems best to leave the lan-guage intact, in case they do.

In another rhyme—

> Gray goose and gander,
> Waft your wings together,
> And carry the good king's daughter
> Over the one-strand river

—that "one-strand" river may be a hint that the poem had its first life as a knitting song, even as an instruction for a particular stitch, but the poems work best if the mystery stays half-hidden. We don't need to know exactly who Jumping Joan is—

> Hinx, minx, the old witch winks,
> The fat begins to fry.
> There's no one home, but Jumping Joan
> And mother and father and I.

—as long as mother and father are safely on the scene.

So, a child's library begins with Mother Goose, and, I think, right next to it should be a songbook. For a couple of reasons. One is that it's as much a pleasure for parents and children to sing as to read together, and another is that there is more American folklore in the songs and so it adds our own historical experience to the English world of Mother Goose. And the logic of the songs belongs to the same magical world. The demise of the miner's daughter Clementine, for example:

> Ruby lips above the water,
> Blowing bubbles soft and fine;
> But alas she was no swimmer,
> So he lost his Clementine.

Selecting the books is probably a matter of price and taste in illustration. One of the tireless collectors and editors of these poems is Iona Opie, a folklorist and scholar of children's games and rhymes, who, together with her late husband Peter Opie, has edited a number of classic children's books. This season she is back with a brand-new *My Very First Mother Goose* (Candlewick) illustrated, with lots of furry cats and bunny rabbits, by Rosemary Wells. It's a delicious collection and it includes most of the old standards—"Hey diddle diddle" and "Jack be nimble" and "Hickety pickety, my black hen"—and also introduces one rhyme from American folklore, "Shoo fly, don't bother me." There is also a lively *Mother Goose* (Oxford) brightly illustrated by Brian Wildsmith, and a number of others. I like the literalness of the late Victorian illustrators. The main thing is that every child should have one and parent and child should have the pleasure of these poems together.

The best songbook I know is *Go In and Out the Window* (Henry Holt), put together by the Metropolitan Museum of Art. It provides the lyrics from several dozen traditional songs, piano arrangements of the tunes, and elegant and surprising illustrations from the museum's collection. The songs range from "Bingo" and "Baa Baa Black Sheep" and "London Bridge" to "Clementine" and "Amazing Grace" and "Sweet Betsy from Pike." The illustrations are unexpected and the more delicious for that. Winslow Homer's painting of a Caribbean palm tree in the wind illustrates Robert Burns's adamantly *Scots* "My Bonnie Lies Over the Ocean," and a Thomas Hart Benton scene of July haying sits next to the African-American spiritual "Nobody Knows the Trouble I've Seen." There also are less expensive songbooks on the market.

Whichever they choose, parents who give their small children the early gift of these traditional songs and poems will have given them a lot of what the culture has to pass on to their unsocialized imaginations.

Other poetry of early childhood: I think of the going-to-bed books I read to my kids until they were as worn as their shreds of blankets and the stuffed animals that were so well handled they were almost effaced of their species markers, making it hard to tell one child's lamb from another's lion. The classics, in my house, were *Goodnight Moon* and *The Little Fur Family,* both of which worked like magic to drift a small child into sleep. The other books my children loved were the four small volumes in Maurice Sendak's Nutshell Library (HarperCollins), which are sold as a boxed set. They especially loved Sendak's story of *Pierre,* the boy who would only say "I don't care." The story has exactly the wildness of a Mother Goose rhyme. Pierre is eaten by a lion; his parents come home, hear "I don't care" from the lion's belly—"Pierre's in there," the father cries—and, by giving the lion a good shake, makes his disgorge their son. Sendak's other beloved books, *Where the Wild Things Are* and *In the Night Kitchen,* belong to the latter part of early childhood and must by now, I think, be on everyone's list of basic books for children.

The poets of middle childhood are Robert Louis Stevenson, Dr. Seuss, and Shel Silverstein. Two generations ago the list would have included a Midwestern poet of the late 19th century, Eugene Field, author of "The Gingham Dog and the Calico Cat" and "Wynken Blynken and Nod." Inexpensive collections of his children's poems are still to be found, but tastes have changed and I think only those two poems have survived in the anthologies. The work of the great English nonsense poet Edward Lear, author of the immortal "Owl and the Pussycat" (which I heard performed as an epithalamium by the wedding party in ensemble at a wedding last summer), is also available. As is the work of Hilaire Belloc, who wrote very funny and slightly sadistic parodies of Victorian moral verse for children, with titles like *Cautionary Verses* and *The Bad Child's Book of Beastly Verses.* But the most popular poets are Stevenson, Dr. Seuss, and Silverstein.

Seuss and Silverstein can be found in any bookstore, and so can various editions of Stevenson's *A Child's Garden of Verses.* How the author of *The Strange Case of Dr. Jekyll and Mr. Hyde* came to write one of the classic books of children's poetry is something of a mystery. The book was published in 1885 when Stevenson was 35 years old, so it must remember his own childhood in the 1850s. It's been said that the Victorians invented childhood, at least the kind of childhood that the idea of a "nursery" evokes, that set-apart middle class world of imagination and anxiety that Peter Pan came out of. Stevenson's poems seem to have expressed that world absolutely. His book was an immediate success, and it's been in print ever since. After Mother Goose, it is probably the best-selling book of children's poetry in the English language. There is an extremely beautiful edition of the book available from Chronicle Books that includes more than a hundred pictures by late 19th- and early 20th-century children's book illustrators that, by themselves, make a quite magical record of the idea of childhood these Victorian poems create.

It's my experience that at about the time they learn to read competently themselves, children become creatures of story. They love prose. This is the time, according to students of children's art, when their drawing becomes more analytic. They start to take pleasure in the stylizations of realistic representation, the sun with its radiant spikes and the box-like house with chimney and smoke. It's a good time to introduce them to more challenging poems. But don't be surprised if they lose interest in poetry altogether. I used to try to keep poetry on the agenda by reading to them, in between the Narnia books of C.S. Lewis and the prairie books of Laura Ingalls Wilder, poems from anthologies of children's verse of the kind that include Stevenson and Belloc, and Fields, but also offer them T.S. Eliot's cats and Shakespeare's songs and poems by Emily Dickinson and Robert Frost, and what I discovered was that they liked the poems best if they read them to me, or memorized and performed them.

The best anthologies, as far as I know, are *The New Oxford Book of Children's Verse,* the shorter *Oxford Treasury of Classic Poems,* and the more recent *A Child's Anthology of Poetry.* The new Oxford anthology, updated by Neil Philip, contains poems literate, various—Gertrude Stein is here, and young American poets like Sandra Cisneros and Janet Wong—and somewhat English in emphasis. *A Child's Anthology of Poetry,* edited by Elizabeth Hauge Sword and Victoria McCarthy (Ecco), was assembled with the help of an advisory board of well-known contemporary poets like Mark Strand and Ishmael Reed and Louise Glück, who were asked what poems they read to their children, and is a little more contemporary and a little more American in emphasis. To my mind it's a fresher look at the idea of children's poetry, but I like both books a lot and think they should be on a child's bookshelf. Parents will have to browse in them to see which they prefer.

A few more books. There is an unexpectedly affecting and interesting volume from Doubleday, Linda Grantham's *In Flanders Field,* that tells the story of one of the most popular poems of World War I. It was written by John McCrae, a Canadian medical officer, after the terrible Second Battle of Ypres in 1915 and the book, hauntingly illustrated by Janet Wilson, manages to tell the story of the war, the battle, the poet, and the making of the poem in vivid and simple prose. To my mind Grantham waffles a little on the horror of that war and the nobility of the poetry, but the art doesn't, and it could send an older child on to the poems of Wilfred Owen and Siegfried Sassoon.

Another very good new prose book is Audrey Osofsky's *Free to Dream* (Lothrop, Lee & Shepard), a biography of Langston Hughes, one of the most important African-American poets of the century. It's full of photographs and posters from the period that catch the feel of Hughes's difficult childhood and the excitement of the years of the Harlem Renaissance. The book does an especially good job of rendering Hughes's early years and it quotes from his poems in a way that will show readers exactly how the poems came out of his life. It's a book that would give children a clear sense of what it was like to be colored in America in the first half of the century, and how that experience made one of our most powerful poets.

The book to read beside the biography is the collection of his own poems, *The Dream Keeper* (Alfred A. Knopf), that Langston Hughes published in 1932. It's been reissued with black-and-white scratchboard illustrations by Brian Pinkney, which catch and modernize the flavor of 1930s book illustration. Some of the poems, written in the 1920s, have the flavor of the blues and the work song and the gospel song, some of them are satiric and some dreamy, and a few have that magical simplicity that belongs equally to the blues, the folk song and the poetry of childhood. Like this one, for example:

POEM

I loved my friend.
He went away from me.
There's nothing more to say.
The poem ends,
Soft as it began—
I loved my friend.

This has the inevitability of a nursery rhyme. It does what poetry does. And it does it with a quiet attitude toward exact rhyme that modernist poetry shared with the blues: "me" and "say," "ends" and "began" and "friend."

So much energy and pleasure to be shared. And the best thing about the poetry and songs is that you can keep going back to them. In Maurice Sendak's *Pierre,* it was the moment of Pierre's emergence from the lion's belly that my children liked to hear over and over again. The very energy of the philosopher's "ungraspable rhythm" of life is in it:

> He rubbed his eyes and scratched his head
> And laughed because he wasn't dead.

You could hardly put the matter more plainly.

---

One of the most beautiful children's books published for the Christmas season is a collection of mostly turn-of-the-last-century translations of traditional Native American songs, accompanied by some of the photographs of Edward S. Curtis, who between 1898 and 1930 made the most complete photographic record we have of Native American life. The book, *Earth Always Endures: Native American Poems* (Viking), was edited by Neil Philips; he had the tact not to try to rewrite the transcriptions of the songs by early ethnologists and musicologists and students of Native American language, which have a simplicity that later efforts to turn them into 20th-century poems for children always manage to spoil.

Here, for example, is the transcription of a Navajo song by Washington Matthews, an Irish surgeon who served in the U.S. 7th Cavalry and later studied Navajo:

MAGPIE SONG

The magpie! The magpie! Here underneath
In the white of his wings are the footsteps of morning.
It dawns! It dawns!

And here are some songs transcribed by Frances Densmore, a re-
markable self-trained student of Native American music, who, in the
course of studying Chippewa, Hidatsa, and Sioux music, made these
early translations of these songs:

SONG OF THE THUNDERS

Sometimes
I go about pitying
myself
while I am carried by the wind
across the sky.

SONG OF THE TREES

The wind
only
I am afraid of.

THE NOISE OF THE VILLAGE

Whenever I pause
the noise
of the village.

BROWN OWLS

Brown owls come here in the blue evening.
They are hooting about.
They are shaking their wings and hooting.

Densmore's *Chippewa Music* was published in 1910. She used inden-
tations and line breaks to indicate the phrasing patterns of the songs, and

they make poems that look startlingly like the imagistic free verse that American poets in New York and London would be experimenting with a few years later.

The combination of Curtis's sepia photographs and these plain versions of the songs, made when many of them were disappearing, catches a moment in American history when European Americans were belatedly trying to understand and record the traditional ways of life they had, often violently, displaced. It makes for a vivid and beautiful book that is somehow not merely elegiac; it brings into the present these oldest songs of our relation to the American earth.

# WINTER

Christmas carols seem to come from nowhere, but some of the best known derive from the hymn tradition of Victorian America. One of them is "O Little Town of Bethlehem." It was written by Phillips Brooks (1835–1893), an Episcopal priest, born in Boston and educated at Harvard, who was rector of the Church of the Holy Trinity in Philadelphia. An eloquent speaker, he was, as an old man, invited to preach at Westminster Abbey and before Queen Victoria at Windsor. He came to public attention when he was invited to compose a prayer for the Harvard Commemoration of the Civil War Dead in 1865. A year later he wrote "O Little Town of Bethlehem" for his Sunday school. It was first performed by children in Philadelphia at Christmas in 1868.

This explains something to me about the power of the song, especially its exquisite first stanza. It is a poem about Christmas and about peace written when the butchery at Shiloh and Gettysburg and Bull Run was still a wound in public memory, and it carries, in the aftermath of that war, the intensity of the yearning for peace. Poignant for us, because Bethlehem continues, in our time, to be a focus of that longing. The hymn is written in the common meter—alternating eight and six syllable lines, the same measure Emily Dickinson used, with the shorter second and fourth lines rhyming. It's interesting to read the hymn as a poem—in the tradition that produced "Rock of Ages" and "Amazing Grace" and "Shall We Gather at the River?"—when you know its historical context. Here it is:

O LITTLE TOWN OF BETHLEHEM

O little town of Bethlehem!
How still we see thee lie,
Above thy deep and dreamless sleep,
The silent stars go by;
Yet in thy dark streets shineth
The Everlasting light;
The hopes and fears of all the years,
Are met in thee tonight.

For Christ is born of Mary,
And gathered all above,
While mortals sleep the angels keep
Their watch of wondering love.
O morning stars together
Proclaim the holy birth!
And praises sing to God the King,
And peace to men on earth.

How silently, how silently,
The wondrous gift is given;
So God imparts to human hearts
The blessings of His heaven.
No ear may hear his coming,
But in this world of sin,
Where meek souls will receive him still,
The dear Christ enters in.

O holy child of Bethlehem!
Descend to us, we pray,
Cast out our sin and enter in,
Be born in us to-day.
We hear the Christmas angels,
The great glad tidings tell,
O, come to us, abide with us,
Our Lord Emmanuel!

"Wondering love" is another striking phrase. We must give the angels a lot to wonder about. Happy holiday!

"Auld Lang Syne" is, of course, a phrase from a poem of Robert Burns; it means, roughly, "the good old days." But, less roughly, it's a little more complicated than that. "Syne" is a Scots and north British dialect word that meant something like "since," as in "long since," but it also had the meaning of "next after that," as in "soon or syne," "sooner or later." The Oxford English dictionary gives a 15th-century expression: "First to lofe and syne to lak": "First to loaf and the very next one to lack." What I like about this is that it gives the phrase from Burns a turn. He didn't invent it; it was a colloquial expression, and it seems to have meant something like "the old what-comes-next."

Here's a New Year's poem by Maxine Kumin, a Pulitzer Prize winner and a former Consultant in Poetry to the Library of Congress. I should tell you that when she was a young woman, Kumin studied poetry in Boston with Robert Lowell, and two of her classmates were Sylvia Plath and Anne Sexton, both of whom went on to fame and suicide. Maxine Kumin was the survivor among those gifted young writers.

So here's a cup of kindness for the old what-happens-next. It's from Kumin's new book, *Connecting the Dots,* published by Norton.

NEW YEAR'S EVE 1959
*remembering Anne Sexton and Jack Geiger*

This was the way we used to party:
lamps unplugged, shoved in the closet
rugs rolled up, furniture pushed back
Glenn Miller singles on the spindle.

There was the poet kicking off her shoes
to jitterbug with the Physician
for Social Responsibility
the only time they ever met

and he pecking his head to the beat
swinging her out on the stalk of his arm
setting all eight gores of her skirt
twirling, then hauling her in for a Fred

Astaire session of deep dips
and both of them cutting out to strut
humming along with the riffs
that punctuated "Chattanooga Choo Choo."

This was after Seoul and before Saigon.
Coke was still a carbonated drink
we added rum to. There was a French wine
but someone had misplaced the curlicue

and a not-yet famous novelist
magicked the cork out on the hinge
of the back door to "Sunrise Serenade"
and dance was the dark enabler.

Lights off a long minute at midnight
(squeals and false moans) madcap Anne
long-dead now and Jack snowily
balding who led the drive to halt the bomb

and I alone am saved to tell you
how they could jive.

---

The public schools in California, especially the schools attended by the urban poor, are brutally overcrowded, understaffed, and underfunded, so people are doing the intelligent thing and having a debate about whether a dialect spoken by some African-Americans is a language. (A language, as George Bernard Shaw wisely observed, is a dialect with an army.)

The play between dialects—between African-American speech patterns and the language most literature gets written in—is one of the sources of tension and aesthetic invention in African-American poetry.

More than most, African-American poets have had to figure out whether they were speaking for themselves personally or for their community, and the tensions in this choice are one of the fascinations of the work of Amiri Baraka, who began his literary life as a Greenwich Village poet named LeRoi Jones and wrote a version of Beat poetry in the 1950s and early 1960s, as well as several remarkable plays, including "Dutchman" and "The Slave," one of the best experimental novels of the period—*The System of Dante's Hell,* and the best single book about the culture that gets expressed in the blues—*Blues People.* In the late '60s Jones changed his name to Baraka and began to write a publicly committed, political, black poetry. The title of his selected poems, *Transbluesency: The Selected Poems of Amiri Baraka/LeRoi Jones (1961–1995),* is a wonderful chance to think about or read for the first time the work of this central, often troubling, poet of the '50s and '60s generation.

Here, from that book, is a small late poem that muses on language. It's from a sequence called "Wise," a word that means one thing in standard English and another—something like "wised up"—in the language of the street:

WISE 3

Son singin
fount some
words./ Son
singin
in that other
language
talkin bout "bay
bee, why you
leave me
here," talkin bout
"up unner de sun
cotton in my hand." Son
singing, think he bad
cause he
can speak

they language, talkin bout
"dark was the night
the ocean deep
white eyes cut through me
made me weep."

Son singin
fount some words. Think
he bad. Speak
they
language.
'sawright
I say
'sawright
wit me
look like
yeh, we gon be here
a taste.

This could be about the Mississippi delta bluesman, Son House, but it is also about himself, I think, who began to "fount" words in his prolific early years. (You can't tell if this is dialect or a Joycean pun on "found" and "fount.") It's a peculiarity of American life that we all comfort ourselves with the blues—songs made of what the Europeans among our ancestors inflicted on the Africans among our ancestors to make our most characteristic folk poetry. I think I'm going to be saying to myself for a while, when things go bad, "'sawright, look like we gon be here a taste."

---

H ere are some winter haiku. In classical Japanese poetry, winter is the season of the world stripped bare. Since, in theory at least, each haiku is supposed not only to illuminate a moment but make an image of the way life is, winter is usually the season of irreducible realities. But in practice Japanese poets use winter imagery in a striking variety of ways. Here are three by Bashō:

> First snow
> falling
> on a half-finished bridge.

Probably a good New Year's poem: fresh snow and the unfinished project of our lives. I haven't, as you see, tried to keep the 17-syllable count in these translations.

> A snowy morning—
> by myself
> chewing on dried salmon.

Dried salmon is an ordinary breakfast, neither rich nor poor. The cultural translation would probably be corn flakes.

> Winter solitude
> in a world of one color,
> the sound of wind.

Here are three by the 19th-century poet-painter Buson, whose work is often visually intense:

> Straw sandal half sunk
> in an old pond
> in the sleety snow.

> Blow of an ax,
> scent of pine:
> the winter woods.

A tethered horse,
snow
in both stirrups.

And here are three by Issa, whose way with the form was often hu-
morous:

No talent
and so no sin—
a winter day.

From the end of the nose
of the Buddha on the moor
hang icicles.

As if even he has a cold. This next one is probably about karma, about
the fact that every action has an effect, but also about finding small things
to be interested in even in the bleakness of winter.

Pissing in the snow
outside my door—
it makes a very straight hole.

These versions can be found in *The Essential Haiku* (edited by Robert
Hass, Ecco Press).

---

Poets, of course, have had their say about inaugurations
and about presidents over the years. There is the great in-
dignation in Robert Duncan's masterful "Poem Begin-
ning with a Line from Pindar," which reels off names with prophetic
intensity:

Harding, Wilson, Taft, Roosevelt,
idiots fumbling at the bride's door,
hear the cries of men in meaningless debt and war.
Where among these did the spirit reside
that restores the land to productive order?
McKinley, Cleveland, Harrison, Arthur,
Garfield, Hayes, Grant, Johnson
dwell in the roots of the heart's rancor.

And there is Robert Lowell's "Inauguration Day: January 1953."
The poem appeared in *Life Studies,* which is one of the three or four most
influential books of American poetry published in this half-century.
Lowell was an ardent supporter of Adlai Stevenson and expressed his
unhappiness with the results of the 1952 election in a sort of truncated
Miltonic sonnet (four beats to the line rather than the grander five) in
which he meditates on the installation of one American general at the
tomb of another.

INAUGURATION DAY: JANUARY 1953

The snow had buried Stuyvesant.
The subways drummed the vaults. I heard
the El's green girders charge on Third,
Manhattan's truss of adamant,
that groaned in ermine, slummed on want . . .
Cyclonic zero of the word,
Cod of our armies, who interred
Cold Harbor's blue immortals, Grant!
Horseman, your sword is in the groove!

Ice, ice. Our wheels no longer move.
Look, the fixed stars, all just alike
as lackland atoms, split apart,
and the Republic summons Ike,
the mausoleum in her heart.

"Cold Harbor" was one of the worst Union defeats of the Civil War and not General Grant's finest moment. Lowell's poem can be found in *Life Studies* and *For the Union Dead,* a paperback volume from Farrar, Straus & Giroux that puts together two of his best books. Robert Duncan's "Poem" is in his *Selected Poems* from New Directions.

---

Poets talk to poets in their poems. The new book by Washington, D.C.'s Henry Taylor, his first since the Pulitzer Prize-winning *The Flying Changes* of 1986, contains a sonnet about Edwin Arlington Robinson, who wrote sonnets about a number of writers, including the early-19th-century narrative poet George Crabbe and the French novelist Emile Zola. Robinson was a New Englander, perhaps the best, certainly the toughest American poet in the years just before the appearance of Robert Frost and T.S. Eliot. Robinson—down on his luck and desperately poor in 1903—got some help from the president of the United States. Theodore Roosevelt wrote him a fan letter about his third book, *Captain Craig,* in that year and found Robinson a job in the New York Customs House, where Herman Melville had worked before him. Here is Robinson's sonnet on Crabbe:

GEORGE CRABBE

Give him the darkest inch your shelf allows,
Hide him in lonely garrets, if you will,—
But his hard human pulse is throbbing still
With the sure strength that fearless truth endows.
In spite of all fine science disavows,
Of his plain excellence and stubborn skill
There yet remains what fashion cannot kill,
Though years have thinned the laurel from his brows.

Whether or not we read him, we can feel
From time to time the vigor of his name

Against us like a finger for the shame
And emptiness of what our souls reveal
In books that are as altars where we kneel
To consecrate the flicker, not the flame.

And here is Taylor's sonnet on Robinson:

AT THE GRAVE OF E.A. ROBINSON

Decades of vague intention drifted by
before I brought small thanks for your large voice—
a bunch of hothouse blooms and Queen Anne's lace
and four lines from "The Man Against the Sky."
My poems, whatever they do, will not repay
the debt they owe to yours, so I let pass
a swift half hour, watching the wind distress
the fringes of my fragile, doomed bouquet.

I beg your pardon, sir. You understood
what use there is in standing here like this,
speaking to one who hears as well as stone;
yet though no answer comes, it does me good
to sound aloud, above your resting place,
hard accents I will carry to my own.

---

Janus, who presides over January, is a two-faced god. He's a gatekeeper, looking backward and forward at the same time. So for February here is a poem about looking forward purely. Well, not so purely. Intensely.

It comes from a first book with a delicious title—*The Lord and the General Din of the World*. The author, Jane Mead, has lived in the wine country of California, went to Vassar and then to the University of Iowa. There is a mood—connected to solitude—that is not loneliness and not despair, but that feels like it could turn into either if you did not try to love the world, or at least look at it attentively. This book seems written from that place. It's a book to be read slowly and quietly, if you are to feel your way into its deep sadness and its small, sudden well of joy. Here's the last poem in the book:

### PASSING A TRUCK FULL OF CHICKENS AT NIGHT ON HIGHWAY EIGHTY

What struck me first was their panic.

Some were pulled by the wind from moving
to the ends of the stacked cages,
some had their heads blown through the bars—

and could not get them in again.
Some hung there like that—dead—
their own feathers blowing, clotting

in their faces. Then
I saw the one that made me slow some—
I lingered there beside her for five miles.

She had pushed her head through the space
between bars—to get a better view.
She had the look of a dog in the back

of a pickup, that eager look of a dog
who knows she's being taken along.
She craned her neck.

She looked around, watched me, then
strained to see over the car—strained
to see what happened beyond.

*That* is the chicken I want to be.

Some very good books are published by small presses and may be hard to find in bookstores. This one is worth the effort. It's published by Sarabande Books in Louisville, Ky.

---

Adventurous readers of poetry were fans of the Canadian writer Michael Ondaatje before he ever turned his hand to prose. Thanks to the success of the film version of his novel *The English Patient,* his selected poems have just appeared from an American publisher. The book is called *The Cinnamon Peeler* (Vintage, 1997). Here, for St. Valentine's Day, is the title poem:

## THE CINNAMON PEELER

If I were a cinnamon peeler
I would ride your bed
and leave the yellow bark dust
on your pillow.

Your breasts and shoulders would reek
you could never walk through markets
without the profession of my fingers
floating over you. The blind would
stumble certain of whom they approached
though you might bathe
under rain gutters, monsoon.

Here on the upper thigh
at this smooth pasture
neighbour to your hair
or the crease
that cuts your back. This ankle.
You will be known among strangers
as the cinnamon peeler's wife.

I could hardly glance at you
before marriage
never touch you
—your keen nosed mother, your rough brothers.
I buried my hands
in saffron, disguised them
over smoking tar,
helped the honey gatherers . . .

When we swam once
I touched you in water
and our bodies remained free,
you could hold me and be blind of smell.
You climbed the bank and said

    this is how you touch other women
the grass cutter's wife, the lime burner's daughter.
And you searched your arms
for the missing perfume

and knew

what good is it
to be the lime burner's daughter
left with no trace
as if not spoken to in the act of love
as if wounded without the pleasure of a scar.

You touched
your belly to my hands
in the dry air and said
I am the cinnamon
peeler's wife. Smell me.

American readers, if they know Chinese poetry at all, know the classic poets of the T'ang Dynasty, Tu Fu and Li Po, who have been translated often in this century. Now contemporary Chinese poetry is beginning to be translated, mostly in the wake of the events in Tiananmen Square in June 1989. An aspect of the democracy movement that spawned those events was the appearance of a new literature. The new poetry took its name from the official critics who complained that it was "misty," by which they meant obscure, sub-jective, smelling suspiciously of personal freedom.

Many of these poets are now in exile in England and France and the United States, including one of the leaders of the movement, Bei Dao, who is now 45 years old and a visiting professor at the University of Cal-ifornia at Davis. Some of Bei Dao's poetry of the 1970s was political. "They say the Ice Age ended years ago," he wrote. "Why are there ici-cles everywhere?" But mostly he troubled the literary establishment be-cause his poems weren't political. They did not seem to shoulder the social task at all. Like classical Chinese poets, but with a 20th-century strangeness, he wrote a poetry of pure attention. Here, for example, is a poem from his most recent book to appear in English, *Landscape Over Zero* (New Directions), translated by David Hinton. As you'll see, the poem feels as if it follows the pulse of consciousness, as it moves from metaphor to metaphor, thought to thought, something like a pilot light turned down to the jets and flickers of a single, intense, blue flame. It's a winter poem, I think, and a poem of exile:

FEBRUARY

night approaching perfection
I float amid languages
the brasses in death's music
full of ice
who's up over the crack in day
singing, water turns bitter
bled flames pale
leaping like leopards toward stars
to dream

you need a form
in the cold morning
an awakened bird
comes closer to the truth
as I and my poems
sink together
february in the book:
certain movements and shadows.

*Landscape Over Zero* is Bei Dao's fourth book to appear in English. The others are also published by New Directions, and the first, *The August Sleepwalker*, will give you the poet as he was first introduced in this country in 1990. There are two very good anthologies that interested readers will want to consult: *Out of the Howling Storm: The New Chinese Poetry*, edited by Tony Barnstone (Wesleyan University Press), and *A Splintered Mirror: Chinese Poetry From the Democracy Movement*, translated by Donald Finkel (North Point).

---

I was looking for a groundhog poem and didn't find one. No groundhog. But I did find one of the best and most readable anthologies of poetry I've come across in a long time. It's Stephen Mitchell's *Bestiary: An Anthology of Poems About Animals*, published by a press called Frog, Ltd. Half of the book is 20th-century masters: Rilke, Neruda, D.H. Lawrence, William Carlos Williams, Elizabeth Bishop, Francis Ponge. There isn't a poem in the book that isn't wonderful, and it's eye-opening to see how many extraordinary poems have come from the contemplation of other creatures. Here—in lieu of the groundhog—are a mouse and a bat.

The mouse comes from an early 19th-century poet named John Clare, a farm worker (for whom the way to poetry was a struggle) who wrote extraordinary poems of observation, poems, really, like nothing else in his time. A tender and dreaming man, he spent his last years in a madhouse:

## THE MOUSE'S NEST

I found a ball of grass among the hay
And progged it as I passed and went away;
And when I turned I fancied something stirred,
And turned again and hoped to catch the bird—
When out an old mouse bolted in the wheats
With all her young ones hanging at her teats;
She looked so odd and so grotesque to me,
I ran and wondered what the thing could be,
And pushed the knapweed bunches where I stood;
Then the mouse hurried from the craking brood.
The young ones squeaked, and as I went away
She found her nest again among the hay.
The water o'er the pebbles scarce could run
And broad old cesspools glittered in the sun.

Even if this poem did not have such essential strangeness and that great, mysterious last line, I'd love it for "progged" and "knapweed" and "craking" (which means—the book has notes—"crawling").

Here's a bat from Emily Dickinson:

The Bat is dun, with wrinkled wings—
Like fallow Article—
And not a song pervade his Lips—
Or none perceptible

His small Umbrella quaintly halved
Describing in the air
An arc alike inscrutable
Elate Philosopher.

Deputed from what Firmament—
Of what Astute Abode—
Empowered with what Malignity
Auspiciously withheld—

To his adroit Creator
Ascribe no less the praise—
Beneficent, believe me,
His Eccentricities—

This is sort of the flying rodent version of William Blake's great "The Tyger," about which creature he asks, "What immortal hand or eye / Dare frame thy fearful symmetry?" Dickinson's version is so odd and ironic—"Beneficent, *believe me,* His Eccentricities"—I'm not sure whether it is about a weird Creator or a weird poet. Perhaps it's a self-portrait.

Anyway, this is a book full of wonders.

---

Jane Shore's new book, *Music Minus One* (Picador), is a nominee for the National Book Critics Circle Award in poetry this year. Shore and her husband, the novelist Howard Norman, divide their time between Vermont and Washington. This book is an autobiographical series about growing up Jewish and female in New Jersey (Shore is in her forties). Some of the poems are spiky and funny. Here's one that gets at the kinds of deep sadness we carry around. Its method is like braiding. It starts with the image of those faces of lost children on milk cartons and twines it around the experience of a lost pregnancy. One of the things that's moving about the poem is the way the sudden rhymes at the end almost nail down the painfulness of it:

MISSING

These children's faces printed on a milk carton—
a boy and a girl
smiling for their school photographs;
each head stuck atop a column
of vital statistics:
date of birth, height and weight, color
of eyes and hair.

On a carton of milk.
Half gallon, a quart.
Of what use is the body's
container, the mother weeping milk or tears.

No amount of crying will hold it back
once it has begun its journey
as you bend all night over the toilet,
over a fresh bowl of water.
Coins of blood spattering the tile floor
as though a murder had been committed.

Something wasn't right, they say,
you are lucky.
Too soon to glimpse the evidence
of gender, or to hear a heartbeat.

Put away the baby book, the list of names.
There are four thousand, at least, to choose from.
No need now to know their derivations,
their meanings.

Faces pass you in the supermarket
as you push the wire cart down the aisles.
The police artist flips through pages
of eyes and noses, assembling a face,
sliding the clear cellophane panels into place.

You take a quart of milk.
Face after face,
smiling obedient soldiers,
march in even rows
in the cold glass case.

A reader wrote recently to ask me to identify these lines, which she'd seen quoted somewhere without an indication of source:

But because *truly* being here is so much;
   because everything here
apparently needs us, this fleeting world,
   which in some strange way
keeps calling to us. Us, the most fleeting of all.
*Once* for each thing. Just once; no more.
   And we too,
just once, completely, even if only once:
to have been at one with the earth, seems
   beyond undoing.

The lines are from the German poet Ranier Maria Rilke's "Duino Elegies," which are thought of as one of the great long poems of the 20th century. They were published in the 1920s and this version comes from *The Selected Poetry of Ranier Maria Rilke,* translated by Stephen Mitchell and published by Random House. One of the themes of the poem is the way in which the longing for absolute transcendence, the dream of perfection, pulls us away from our lives. This particular stanza comes early in the Ninth Elegy, which also contains these lines, perhaps among the most famous in modern literature. They follow the ones I've just quoted:

And so we keep pressing on, trying to achieve it,
trying to hold it firmly in our simple hands,

[the "it," I think, is the being here, the having been at one with the earth]

   in our overcrowded gaze, in our speechless heart.
   Trying to become it.—Whom can we give it to?
   We would
hold on to it all, forever . . . Ah, but what can we take along
into that other realm? Not the art of looking,

which is learned so slowly, and nothing that happened here.
   Nothing.
The sufferings, then. And, above all, the heaviness,
and the long experience of love,—just what is wholly
unsayable. But later, among the stars,
what good is it—they are *better* as they are: unsayable.

[the "they" are the angels of longing, beings of pure completeness who
torment us with the desire to be changed, transformed]

For when the traveler returns from the mountain-slopes into the
   valley,
he brings, not a handful of earth, unsayable to others, but instead
some word he has gained, some pure word, the yellow and blue
gentian. Perhaps we are *here* in order to say: house,
bridge, fountain, gate, pitcher, fruit-tree, window—
at most: column, tower. . . . But to *say* them, you must
   understand,
oh to say them *more* intensely than the Things themselves
ever dreamed of existing. Isn't the secret intent
of this taciturn earth, when it forces lovers together,
that inside their boundless emotion all things may shudder with
   joy?
Threshold: what it means for two lovers
to be wearing down, imperceptibly, the ancient threshold of their
   door—
they too, after the many who came before them
and before those to come. . . . lightly.

*Here* is the time for the *sayable, here* is its homeland.
Speak and bear witness.

A couple of years ago the poet James Galvin wrote a prose book, *The Meadow,* about the life in a valley of the Rocky Mountains near Tie Siding, Wyo., and the death of an old rancher. The book struck a nerve. It's beautifully written and seems on its way to becoming one of those small, surprising classics of our regional literature. Now Galvin's poems have appeared in a new collection, *Resurrection Update: Collected Poems 1975–1997,* from Copper Canyon Press. This one is set in that same valley, at the end of fall, with winter coming on:

### AGAINST THE REST OF THE YEAR

The meadow's a dream I'm working to wake to.
The real river flows under the river.
The real river flows
Over the river.
Three fishermen in yellow slickers
Stitch in and out of the willows
And sometimes stand for a long time, facing the water,
Thinking they are not moving.

Thoughts akimbo
Or watching the West slip through our hopes for it,
We're here with hay down,
Starting the baler, and a thunderhead
Stands forward to the east like a grail of milk.

The sky is cut out for accepting prayers.
    Believe me, it takes them all.
Like empty barrels afloat in the trough of a swell
The stupid bales wait in the field.
The wind scatters a handful of yellow leaves
With the same sowing motion it uses for snow.

After this we won't be haying anymore.
Lyle is going to concentrate on dying for a while
And then he is going to die.
The tall native grasses will come ripe for cutting
And go uncut, go yellow and buckle under snow
As they did before for thousands of years.
Of objects, the stove will be the coldest in the house.
The kitchen table will be there with its chairs,
Sugar bowl, and half-read library book.
The air will be still from no one breathing.

The green of the meadow, the green willows,
The green pines, the green roof, the water
Clear as air where it unfurls over the beaver dam
Like it isn't moving.

In the huge secrecy of the leaning barn
We pile the bodies of millions of grasses,
Where it's dark as a church
And the air is the haydust that was a hundred years.
The tin roof's a marimba band and the afternoon goes dark.
Hay hooks clink into a bucket and nest.
Someone lifts his boot to the running board and rests.
Someone lights a cigarette.
Someone dangles his legs off the back of the flatbed
And holds, between his knees, his hands,
As if they weighed fifty pounds.
*Forever* comes to mind, and peaks where the snow stays.

# SPRING

Since I mentioned that I was having trouble finding a poem about groundhogs a couple of weeks ago, my always interesting readers have been letting me know that I had overlooked what is often regarded as a classic American poem, Richard Eberhart's "The Groundhog." The truth is that I am not especially fond of the poem. Its diction seems to me stilted, though Eberhart has written some poems I admire, especially "The Fury of Aerial Bombardment." But I've received more than a dozen copies of the poem in the mail, and I'm going to yield. You can judge for yourselves.

## THE GROUNDHOG

In June, amid the golden fields,
I saw a groundhog lying dead.
Dead lay he; my senses shook,
And mind outshot our naked frailty.
There lowly in the vigorous summer
His form began its senseless change,
And made my senses waver dim
Seeing nature ferocious in him.
Inspecting close his maggots' might
And seething cauldron of his being,
Half with loathing, half with strange love,
I poked him with an angry stick.
The fever arose, became a flame
And Vigour circumscribed the skies,
Immense energy in the sun,
And through my frame a sunless trembling.
My stick had done nor good nor harm.
Then stood I silent in the day
Watching the object, as before;
And kept my reverence for knowledge
Trying for control, to be still,
To quell the passion of the blood;
Until I had bent down on my knees
Praying for joy in the sight of decay.

And so I left; and I returned
In Autumn strict of eye, to see
The sap gone out of the groundhog,
But the bony sodden hulk remained.
But the year had lost its meaning,
And in intellectual chains
I lost both love and loathing,
Mured up in the wall of wisdom.
Another summer took the fields again
Massive and burning, full of life,
But when I chanced upon the spot
There was only a little hair left,
And bones bleaching in the sunlight
Beautiful as architecture;
I watched them like a geometer,
And cut a walking stick from a birch.
It has been three years, now.
There is no sign of the groundhog.
I stood there in the whirling summer,
My hand capped a withered heart,
And thought of China and of Greece,
Of Alexander in his tent;
Of Montaigne in his tower,
Of Saint Theresa in her wild lament.

---

The Lannan Foundation in Los Angeles, dedicated to promoting literature and the visual arts, began a few years ago to give annual awards to writers and one award for lifetime achievement in literature. The lifetime awards have been especially interesting; they cast a very wide eye and are often both unexpected and deserving. This year's honoree, for example, is an 83-year-old Welsh Anglican priest, R.S. Thomas. He is one of the strongest, least known British poets of the second half of the 20th century, who has made remarkable poetry out of the flinty and unforgiving hill country of Wales and an obdurate, existential Christianity. Thomas is a poet I discovered in my twenties and somehow—his books aren't easily available here—stopped reading. I've just returned to his 500-page *Collected Poems, 1945–1990*, published in England by J.M. Dent, and remembered why I had been so struck by these quiet and forceful poems.

Easter is not Thomas's season. He is more likely to write about Christmas, the bare survival of light in the dark of winter. But I found myself drawn to the spring poems. Here is one from 1946:

### COUNTRY CHURCH (MANAFON)

The church stands, built from the river stone,
Brittle with light, as though a breath could shatter
Its slender frame, or spill the limpid water,
Quiet as sunlight, cupped within the bone.

It stands yet. But though soft flowers break
In delicate waves round limbs the river fashioned
With so smooth care, no friendly God has cautioned
The brimming tides of fescue for its sake.

I had to read that second stanza several times before I felt I had got it. Something about Thomas's God being in the brimming and fierce grass and not in the blossoms, I think.

Here is a poem from 1955:

### IN A COUNTRY CHURCH

To one kneeling down no word came,
Only the wind's song, saddening the lips
Of the grave saints, rigid in glass;
Or the dry whisper of unseen wings,
Bats not angels, in the high roof.
Was he balked by silence? He kneeled long.
And saw love in a dark crown

Of thorns blazing, and a winter tree
Golden with fruit of a man's body.

And here, finally, is a more recent poem, from 10 years ago, when Thomas was 73:

APRIL SONG

Withdrawing from the present,
wandering a past that is alive
in books only. In love
with women, outlasted
by their smiles; the richness
of their apparel puts
the poor in perspective.
The brush dipped in blood
and the knife in art
have preserved their value.
Smouldering times: sacked
cities, incinerable hearts,

and the fledgling God
tipped out of his high
nest into the virgin's lap
by the incorrigible cuckoo.

You won't find his books in your bookstore; you'll have to order the *Collected Poems* from your bookseller. (Another fine book is *No Truce With the Furies,* Bloodaxe Books, Ltd.) But it will be worth the trouble to find the art of this quiet man who made a vision of his country and of his struggle with his art and faith.

The New York poet David Lehman's newest book is called *Valentine Place* (Scribner). It's about city life and romantic love. Its style is ironic, shape-shifting, full of trapdoors, absurdist play, desperate wit, narratives that fall away like funhouse floors. Here's a sample:

TOWARD A DEFINITION OF LOVE

I.

Another time they were making love. "It's even better
When you help," she said. That was the second thing
He liked about her: she had memorized hours
Of movie dialogue, as if their life together
In the close apartment, with the street noise,
The crank calls, and the sinister next-door neighbor,
Consisted of roles to be played with panache,
If possible, and with a song in her heart. Was she lying
When she told him she loved him? Or was she
The nude in his bed with her back to him
As if he were a painter in Paris in 1870
And she were a model in Brooklyn in 1992,
And what separated them was a painted ocean
Representing the unbridgeable distance between them,
As between age and youth, Europe and America?
A condition of their romance was its impossibility—
She would have panicked if he had proposed,
Because love was passion consuming itself
Like a flickering cigarette, an ember in an ashtray.

2.

When she went back to sleep, he thought about her
Some more, and what they had done the night before:
Something holy, but with awful consequences,
Like a revolution about to enter its reign of terror.
In the movie, he was the jilted soldier ("don't you still
Love me?") or the Scandinavian philosopher ("he wondered

Why he had to give her up"). But their lines so truly parallel
Though infinite could never meet, and there was no use
Arguing against the despair that had wakened his longing
For her, now that she was gone. There was no way
To make it last, to prolong a moment of such pleasure,
Sweet and intense, that Faust would have bargained away
His soul for it. In public they acted married. One day
She left. She phoned from the road. A morning of tears
In honor of the first morning he had woken up beside her
With the shades rattling in the window, and the rays
Of light seeping weakly into the room, and the noise
Of the kids playing with a ball in the gutter.

---

Charlie Smith is a novelist and poet, a Southerner living in New York City. His newest book, *Before and After* (Norton) is—like so many recent books of American poems—about family. Maybe it's because we have grown mobile and rootless as a people that this subject is so persistent. Maybe it's because we've come to believe that the furies that drive us are the ghosts of what, as children, we sensed to be our parents' unfulfilled desires, so that we have to try to speak those out loud to make an account of ourselves. Here's a poem about that subject.

THE FRONT MAN

My father was a social man, talking,
making change with his voice, making deals,
promising to give you this for that, a courageous host,
unappalled, like a front man for fair weather.
The world moved through him, back and forth;
he experienced life not as gain or loss,
but as a current flowing through. You sense another's hopes
dying in your chest, another's cramped dependence

on a set of platitudes he's learned by rote,
you feel the tug of a stranger's loss
like a hand letting go, rage like a coat of burning fur,
and this you take, as my father did,
as life, evidence of an eternal kingdom,
built up every day from scratch; and if each night,
when you're alone at last, the guests all moaning in their beds,
you come upon a patch where there's nothing,
and nothing in your arsenal of plans and schemes
to make the knots you tie to cross it safely
will hold, still it's only time passing in the night,
only fear running in your head; the emptiness is moving too.

---

If anyone ever had his say, Allen Ginsberg did. And now, af-
ter years of being symbol and icon of the cultural revolution
of the '60s and '70s, bad boy of the Beat Generation, guru
and crown prince of the flower children, he has, as W.H. Auden said of
W.B. Yeats, disappeared into his poems. His early poems have the energy
of someone who has bitten through the leash. They're full of outrage, hu-
mor, apocalyptic idealism, verbal invention, and a curious, steady sanity.

Here is a poem from those early years, in which a young man from
New Jersey in a California supermarket at night dreams of his poet he-
roes, both of them, as it happens, like him, gay, an awkward and mostly
inadmissible fact in 1954. Here he uses his famous long line not for pro-
phetic rage, but to speak into his own loneliness with tender humor and
to pay homage to a beloved poet-father:

A SUPERMARKET IN CALIFORNIA

What thoughts I have of you tonight, Walt Whitman, for I
    walked down the sidestreets under the trees with a headache
    self-conscious looking at the full moon.
In my hungry fatigue, and shopping for images, I went into the

neon fruit supermarket, dreaming of your enumerations!
What peaches and what penumbras! Whole families shopping
   at night! Aisles full of husbands! Wives in the avocados, ba-
   bies in the tomatoes!—and you, Garcia Lorca, what were
   you doing down by the watermelons?

I saw you, Walt Whitman, childless, lonely old grubber, poking
   among the meats in the refrigerator and eyeing the grocery
   boys.
I heard you asking questions of each: Who killed the pork
   chops? What price bananas? Are you my Angel?
I wandered in and out of the brilliant stacks of cans following
   you,
and followed in my imagination by the store detective.
We strode down the open corridors together in our solitary fancy
   tasting artichokes, possessing every frozen delicacy, and never
   passing the cashier.

Where are we going, Walt Whitman? The doors close in an
   hour. Which way does your beard point tonight?
(I touch your book and dream of our odyssey in the supermarket
   and feel absurd.)
Will we walk all night through solitary streets? The trees add
   shade to shade, lights out in the houses, we'll both be lonely.
Will we stroll dreaming of the lost America of love past blue au-
   tomobiles in driveways, home to our silent cottage?
Ah, dear father, graybeard, lonely old courage-teacher, what
   America did you have when Charon quit poling his ferry
   and you got out on a smoking bank and stood watching the
   boat disappear on the black waters of Lethe?

   I like many things about this poem. I particularly like that moment
of musing self-consciousness: "I touch your book and dream of our od-
yssey and feel absurd." This is a moment at which a lot of poets and
would-be poets get defeated by their own embarrassment and preten-

sion. It's a small example of the way in which Ginsberg was not fearless or shameless; he had the usual fears and shames, but he set out to rid himself of them: a ritual purgation by way of risky frankness and humor. That was one of the great impulses of his art and it's why for my generation he was also, and remains, a courage-teacher.

---

I hesitated for about five minutes over the question of whether I should print one of my wife's poems. Not much longer. Brenda Hillman's one of the most original poets I know, and her newest book, her fifth, *Loose Sugar,* is just out from Wesleyan University Press. It's a mysterious book, searching, fragmentary, full of eccentric and experimental forms, and it's about the big mysteries, desire and memory and what it is to have a body in space and time. Hillman has found a voice in these poems as intimate as thought, so that you feel you're almost overhearing consciousness coming into being and taking its bearings. Here is a poem about, I think, the sensation of existing:

TIME'S BODY

—in the middle of the beginning they woke you
from a long sleep;

you could see the edges of the world
being formed, the boundaries
space would make in its eagerness
to be included.

the problem time would have
in its need to be the main thing.

The source of life is not life
but rebellion toward meaning.
When you saw the workers were already busy,

that the list you'd been handed
was usual and impossible

and held it all, and thin
or most, your will
strong as a paper clip

you needed a location
from which to act on your assigned nature

so you chose time:
seed of light,
seed of torment—

---

There's going to be a new saxophone player in Washington. Robert Pinsky, my successor in the office of poet laureate—a distinguished poet, essayist, translator—is reported to be a pretty good tenor sax player. And he has written a poem, a sort of high-spirited ode, to that instrument. Here it is:

GINZA SAMBA

A monosyllabic European called Sax
Invents a horn, walla whirledy wah, a kind of twisted
Brazen clarinet, but with its column of vibrating
Air shaped not in a cylinder but in a cone
Widening ever outward and bawaah spouting
Infinitely upward through an upturned
Swollen golden bell rimmed
Like a gloxinia flowering
In Sax's Belgian imagination

And in the unfathomable matrix

Of mothers and fathers as a genius graven
Humming into the cells of the body
Or cupped in the resonating grail
Of memory changed and exchanged
As in the trading of brasses,
Pearls and ivory, calicos and slaves,
Laborers and girls, two

Cousins in a royal family
Of Niger known as the Birds or Hawks.
In Christendom one cousin's child
Becomes a "favorite negro" ennobled
By decree of the Czar and founds
A great family, a line of generals,
Dandies and courtiers including the poet
Pushkin, killed in a duel concerning
His wife's honor, while the other cousin sails

In the belly of a slaveship to the port
Of Baltimore where she is raped
And dies in childbirth, but the infant
Will marry a Seminole and in the next
Chorus of time their child fathers
A great Hawk or Bird, with many followers
Among them this great-grandchild of the Jewish
Manager of a Pushkin estate, blowing

His American breath out into the wiggly
Tune uncurling its triplets and sixteenths—the Ginza
Samba of breath and brass, the reed
Vibrating as a valve, the aether, the unimaginable
Wires and circuits of an ingenious box
Here in my room in this house built
A hundred years ago while I was elsewhere:

It is like falling in love, the atavistic
Imperative of some one
Voice or face—the skill, the copper filament,
The golden bellful of notes twirling through
Their invisible element from
Rio to Tokyo and back again gathering
Speed in the variations as they tunnel
The twin haunted labyrinths of stirrup
And anvil echoing here in the hearkening
Instrument of my skull.

A gloss might help a little. Pinsky, who is fascinated by the mix of accident and invention that makes the world, likes facts. It is true, for example, that the great Russian poet Pushkin was partly African on his father's side and it is conceivable that he is, therefore, related to the great Birds and Hawks of American jazz, Charlie Parker and Coleman Hawkins and conceivable also that some great Jewish American player, like Stan Getz, is descended from a manager of the Pushkin estate and that the descendant of some other branch of the family, from Pinsk, say, would grow up a poet in New Jersey and write about this chain of possibilities as if it were a run of notes on the gleaming stem of a saxo-phone.

"Ginza Samba" can be found in Pinsky's collected poems, *The Fig-ured Wheel.*

---

S hirley Kaufman is an American poet born in Seattle who, in the middle of her life, married an Israeli scholar and moved to Jerusalem. Her new collection *Roots in the Air: New and Selected Poems* (Copper Canyon Press) traces that complex mi-gration.

I was looking for a poem of hers for this time of high Spring—"and red poppies. / And after the flower-spattered hills / the Dead Sea. Sunlight / peeling off the old skin"—and came across another much more difficult and painful poem. It opens with the story of one young survivor's spring in the death camps, an image which Kaufman has the tact to record very simply, and then, with the boy's act in mind, she makes of it a poignant and harrowing metaphor for poetry.

## BY THE RIVERS

That spring he was fourteen,
sun on the walls, stale air
sweet in Bergen-Belsen for the first time,
he told me he thought of the nurse
who held him when he was small.
He found a corner
where they did not catch him:
rush of the brilliance and the heat
and no one there. He opened his clothes,
hunched over his wasted body,
and made it spill.

The poem wants to look forward, not
back, but out there as far as it can see
are ruins: body of Abel body of god body
of smoke. And no recognizable
child to mourn.

So it begins with longing.
Or with fear, that old dog
stinking beside it, scabby and blind.

And all the time the future
is pushing up uncalled for
under the cold ground, or gliding down
like the first snow, wet syllables
that melt and soak up the darkness.
The poem wants to get out

of where it is. But is instructed
to remember. In shameless daylight.
By the rivers of salt.

---

William Dickey was a poet of the 1950s generation, the one that includes Adrienne Rich, John Ashbery, and the late Allen Ginsberg. He was not among the ones who became especially famous or popular, but he was a much-loved teacher (for many years at San Francisco State University), a rather shy, scholarly, and unfailingly kind man, and, as became increasingly evident in his poetry over the years, he had a great sweetness and playfulness of mind. He died of an AIDS-related illness in 1994, and now his final book has appeared, *The Education of Desire,* from Wesleyan University Press. It is a rich book, written by a man who knew he was dying and who made almost everything around him shine with interest when he turned his attention to it.

The last poem in the book is a kind of invocation to the arrival of summer. Printing it here seems a good way to conjure the summer to come and to honor his memory:

ON THE WHITE ROAD

On the white road
in dust of summer
someone's arriving

apricots bend
from the wall-garden
welcoming summer

someone's arriving
clothed only in light
his hands empty

his eyes full of islands
stroked by blue ocean
in the summer air

violent and singing
on the empty road
someone's arriving

the white light
cherishing his step
and his naked stare.

Further thoughts: I was struck first by this poem because it's beauti⁄
ful; re⁄reading it, I see that the image is full of resonances. It's an invoca⁄
tion of summer as a kind of seasonal god. It seems also to be an evocation
of an ideal lover, or of Eros himself. And it's the last poem in the book: It
may also be about the meeting with death, or about us, the readers, meet⁄
ing the poet when he is finally dressed only in his words.

---

The imagery of American poetry is mostly realistic—
William Carlos Williams's "red wheelbarrow glazed
with rain water beside the white chickens" and Robert
Frost's "my little horse must think it queer to stop without a farmhouse
near between the woods and frozen lake the darkest evening of the year."
The surrealism that became so important to the imagery of European
and Latin American poetry in the 1930s and 1940s was slow to have an
effect in the English⁄speaking world. Now it's everywhere, from rock
lyrics to experimental poetry. It came into American poetry by way of
translation, mostly, and among the most influential translations were
those Robert Bly made in the 1950s and 1960s of Spanish poets. One of
those volumes, *Lorca & Jimenez: Selected Poems,* has just been reissued in
paperback by Beacon Press. It includes Bly's translations of the poems of

New York City by the great Spanish poet Federico Garcia Lorca. Reading them you can see, among other things, the way Lorca's furious and apocalyptic style must have influenced Allen Ginsberg's "Howl" and all the poems that Ginsberg in his turn influenced, including the early lyrics of Bob Dylan.

Here is a section of Lorca's "Dance of Death" in Bly's translation:

Mountain passes of lime were walling in the empty sky;
you heard the voices of those dying under the dung of birds.
A sky, clipped and pure, exactly like itself,
with the fluff and sharp-edged lily of its invisible mountains,

has killed the most delicate stems of song,
and gone off to the flood crowded with sap,
across the resting time of the final marchers,
lifting bits of mirror with its tail.

While the Chinaman was crying on the roof
without finding the nakedness of his wife,
and the bank president was watching the pressure-gauge
that measures the remorseless silence of money,
the black mask was arriving at Wall Street.

This vault that makes the eyes turn yellow
is not an odd place for dancing.
There is a wire stretched from the Sphinx to the safety deposit
    box
that passes through the heart of all poor children.
The primitive energy is dancing with the machine energy,
in their frenzy wholly ignorant of the original light.
Because if the wheel forgets its formula,
it might as well sing naked with the herds of horses;
and if a flame burns up the frozen plans
the sky will have to run away from the roar of the windows.

This place is a good place for dancing, I say this truth,
the black mask will dance between columns of blood and
   numbers,
between downpours of gold and groans of unemployed workers
who will go howling, dark night, through your time without
   stars.
O savage North America! shameless! savage,
stretched out on the frontier of the snow!

Bly translated Lorca's *"el chino"* as "the Chinaman" probably to get
the flavor of American English circa 1930. I don't think anybody is
comfortable with that term. In this passage, however, it catches some-
thing of Lorca's sense of immigrant displacement and grief.

---

A reader wrote last winter to ask if I would comment on a
poem by John Keats, "Daisy's Song," and wondered if
Keats had been influenced by the poems of William
Blake. It's a charming poem, and this is the season to print it.

For Keats it's an early poem. All of Keats's poems are early—he died
at the age of 26. He wrote this one in February of 1818 when he was 22,
and it appears in the *Collected Poems,* the splendid Penguin Classics edi-
tion edited by John Bernard, with a group of other poems under the title
"Extracts from an Opera." He may have been trying his hand at writing
a libretto. It would have included this little song:

DAISY'S SONG
I

The sun, with his great eye,
Sees not as much as I;
And the moon, all silver-proud,
Might as well be in a cloud.

II

And O the spring—the spring!
I lead the life of a king!
Couched in the teeming grass,
I spy each pretty lass.

III

I look where no one dares,
And I stare where no one stares,
And when the night is nigh,
Lambs bleat my lullaby.

A late spring, early summer poem, immensely and cheerfully sweet.
I suppose, if it has a symbolic meaning, it would have to do with a kind
of earthy imagination, different from the sun (God?) and the moon
(Wisdom? the Ideal? Something like that—Keats was in the process of
finishing his long poem "Endymion," which is about falling in love
with a high, cloudy kind of beauty). To my rather literal mind it seems
to be about being able to look up girls' dresses, and in this way it proba-
bly is closer in sensibility to Robert Burns than William Blake. Blake
took these little song forms, some of them borrowed from the hymns in
Protestant churches, some of them from Renaissance song, and made vi-
sionary poems like the "Ah! Sunflower" and "The Sick Rose." But, ac-
cording to the scholars, there seems to be no evidence, as surprising as it
is, that Keats ever read Blake.

My impression is that Keats was probably trying to catch the playful,
un-Puritanical spirit of 16th-century song. There's another poem he
wrote around this time that also suggests this state of mind. It's called
"Where be ye going, you Devon maid?" The last stanza goes like this:

I'll put your basket all safe in a *nook*,
And your shawl I hang up *on this willow*,
And we will sigh in the daisy's eye
And kiss on a grass-green pillow.

Sighing in the daisy's eye: It sounds like a prescription for summer.

One of the strongest new books I've read in the last year or so is Jon Davis's *Scrimmage of Appetite*. It was pub⁄lished by University of Akron Press, so your book⁄seller might not have it, but it's worth ordering. Davis teaches at the In⁄stitute of American Indian Arts in Santa Fe, and this is his second book. Here's a prose poem:

BLUES

*Forms seek subjects.*
   —Frank Bidart

The first line must be about heartbreak: "Oh, she stomped my heart / give me the stompin' blues." The second must be the first sung with increasing rage and despair: "Yeah, she STOMPED my heart / gi' me the STOMPIN' blues." The third must add detail and complete the breakage: "She stomped it with my best friend / wore my favorite shoes."

At this point, the guitar may complain or cry. At this point, the singer may moan, "Oh, baby." At this point, a white boy, a construction laborer in work boots and flannel shirt may, having been overcome by the poignancy of the occasion and several draught beers, begin to sway and shout "Amen!" thrusting his plastic cup into the air.

Which may or may not signal the coming of an avant⁄garde. Say the next time he shouts, "Radiator!" Say the next time he shouts, "Come unto the Lord." Say the next time he shouts, "I'm on fire" or "Stuff the turkey. The kids are in the car and I can't stay long." Say he talks over the bridge, saying, "The cake flopped. The cake flopped. We gave it to the cousin who eats such things."

Say he begins rocking vigorously and continues: "The linoleum's cracking by the fridge. When the welfare lady comes be neat, be clean, but don't be happy. Tell her we never have enough. Tell her we behave anyway. After dark, if we lean the brick palette against the back wall and climb it like a ladder and pull ourselves onto the back porch where the door is always open, we can go inside."

At this point, the guitarist may attack a single note and hold it. "We'll bring a flashlight—a small one—and we'll eat ice cream and cheese and steal the records—Love, Steppenwolf, *The Soft Parade, Dr. Byrd and Mr. Hyde.* When I call your brand of cigarettes, the brand you're thinking of, you run around the yard and I'll try to catch you. Darkness. Toads along the porch. Katydids creaking. Bats. One night we shined a flashlight into the maple and watched small animals hurl themselves onto the roof of the house. Flying squirrels."

He might also mention the way those bats flew—the veering, the way they swooped at the stones he tossed. The stones he gathered from the driveway where the Dugan man parked his bread truck. It would be nearly dark, and he'd climb in the open door with his brothers and eat cherry pies while the Dugan man drank coffee with his grandmother. Then they'd slip out the side door and the bats would be veering above.

Attraction and avoidance. This is the blues. It keeps repeating itself. Keeps repeating its lonesome self. The object is purgation. Catharsis. The object is triumph. Endurance. Humor. At this point, the singer may shout, "Hurt me!" And the guitar may answer, *Pain, pain, pain. Pain, pain, pain.*

# SUMMER

For the June of weddings, one of the oldest cycles of love songs in the Western tradition: *The Song of Songs.* There is a new translation by the poet Chana Bloch and the Hebrew scholar Ariel Bloch, published by Random House. Scholars think these songs were probably written down in the third century B.C.E. around the time of Alexander the Great. Whether they are an original work by a single author or a group of ancient folk songs stitched together is a matter of dispute. But it seems clear that they are a cycle of poems, a dialogue between a bridegroom and a bride. No one argues about their sensuous freshness and beauty. The Blochs have divided the work up into individual lyrics, based on what is the most authoritative scholarly guesswork.

Scholarship aside, these poems are for the brides and grooms. I'll give you the Blochs' translation first and then the King James. Here is the bridegroom:

> Oh come with me, my bride,
> come down with me from Lebanon.
> Look down from the peak of Amana,
> look down from Senir and Hermon,
> from the mountains of the leopards,
> the lion's den.
>
> You have ravished my heart,
> my sister, my bride,
> ravished me with one glance of your eyes,
> one link of your necklace.
>
> And oh, your sweet loving,
> my sister, my bride.
> The wine of your kisses, the spice
> of your fragrant oils.
>
> Your lips are honey, honey and milk
> are under your tongue,
> your clothes hold the scent of Lebanon.

(Song, 4:8, "Come with me from Lebanon, my spouse, with me from Lebanon: look from the top of Amana, of Shenir and Hermon, from the lions' dens, from the mountains of the leopards. Thou hast ravished my heart, my sister, my spouse; thou hast ravished my heart with one of thine eyes, with one chain of thy neck. How fair is thy love, my sister, my spouse! How much better is thy love than wine! and the smell of thine ointments than all spices! Thy lips, O my spouse, drop as the honeycomb; honey and milk are under thy tongue; and the smell of thy garments is like the smell of Lebanon.")

Here is the bride, according to the Blochs:

Come, my beloved,
let us go out into the fields
and lie all night among the flowering henna.

Let us go early to the vineyards
to see if the vine has budded,
if the blossoms have opened
and the pomegranate is in flower.

There I will give you my love.

The air is filled with the scent of mandrakes
and at our doors
rare fruit of every kind, my love,
I have stored away for you.

(Song, 7:12, "Come, my beloved, let us go forth into the field; let us lodge in the villages. Let us get up early to the vineyards; let us see if the vine flourish, whether the tender grape appear and the pomegranate bud forth: there will I give thee my loves. The mandrake give a smell and at our gates are all manner of pleasant fruits, new and old, which I have laid up for thee, O my beloved.")

W.S. Merwin recently won the very handsome Tan-
ning Prize, an award given to a writer who is consid-
ered an American master. Born in New Jersey, a
Princeton graduate, an activist in the years of the civil rights movement
and the Vietnam War, Merwin as a young man in the 1950s wrote daz-
zling, complex, mythic poems. He now lives in Hawaii and grows a
plantation of native palms. Over the years his work has gotten simpler
and more mysterious. Here are some poems from a suite called "Summer
Canyon." They appear in the recently published *Flower and Hand: Poems
1977–83,* published by Copper Canyon, that makes a good selection of
work in the later style:

SUMMER CANYON

Some of the mayflies
drift on into June
without their names

———

Spring reappears in the evening
oyster cloud sky catches in pines
water light wells out of needles after sundown

———

On small summit pine hollow
field chickweed under trees
split white petals drifting over shadows

———

Two crows call to each other
flying over
same places

———

Three broad blue petals
I do not know
what kind of flower

———

Leaves never seen before
look how they have grown
since we came here

————

Day's end green summer stillness
pine shadows drift far out
on long boards

————

Mourning dove sound
cricket sound
no third

————

All day the wind blows
and the rock
keeps its place

————

Sunlight after rain
reflections of ruffled water
cross the ceiling

————

High in the east full moon
and far below on the plain
low clouds and lightning

————

Jay clatters through dark pines
it remembers
something it wants among them

I once heard Merwin read poems like these. Someone in the audi-
ence asked if they were haiku. He said, no, and then gave a definition of
haiku: seventeen-syllable poems, written in Japanese.

Some poets' styles are so distinctive that, if you found a scrap of a poem blowing in the wind and picked it up and read a few lines, you'd know who wrote it. (Coleridge said he could recognize lines by Wordsworth that way.) C.K. Williams is another of those poets. His stylistic signature is a very long line. The standard "long line" in English poetry is 10 syllables. Though Whitman stretched it out, and other free verse poets have since, they mostly use it occasionally, to create the sense of an ecstatic rush of breath. Williams uses the long line analytically. It often runs to about 22 syllables—twice the traditional line, and longer. It gives him a broad canvas on which to work and gives his poems some of the virtues of prose. His work is often to understand what he sees. You can feel him, as he works, struggling for exactness, comprehension. It makes him, I think, one of the most interesting poets now writing. It's hard to convey the range of things he can do with his form. You can get that from his *Selected Poems* (Farrar, Straus & Giroux), but here's an example from his most recent book *The Vigil* (also Farrar, Straus & Giroux):

INSTINCT

Although he's apparently the youngest (his little Rasta-beard is
    barely down and feathers),
most casually connected (he hardly glances at the girl he's with,
    though she might be his wife),
half-sloshed (or more than half) on picnic-whiskey teen-aged
    father, when his little son,
two or so, tumbles from the slide, hard enough to scare himself,
    hard enough to make him cry,
really cry, not partly cry, not pretend the fright for what must be
    some scarce attention,
but really let it out, let loudly be revealed the fear of having been
    so close to real fear,
he, the father, knows just how quickly he should pick the child
    up, then how firmly hold it,
fit its head into the muscled socket of his shoulder, rub its back,
    croon and whisper to it,

and finally pull away a little, about a head's length, looking, still
    concerned, into its eyes,
then smiling, broadly, brightly, as though something had been
    shared, something of importance,
not dreadful, or not very, not at least now that it's past, but rather
    something . . . funny,
funny, yes, it was funny, wasn't it, to fall and cry like that, though
    one certainly can understand,
we've all had glimpses of a premonition of the anguish out there,
    you're better now, though,
aren't you, why don't you go back and try again, I'll watch you,
    maybe have another drink,
yes, my son, my love, I'll go back and be myself now: you go be
    the person you are, too.

---

The summer movies are so bad, there may be no solution but poems about movies. Here is the late Howard Moss on his affection for old horror films:

## HORROR MOVIE

Dr. Unlikely, we love you so,
You who made the double-headed rabbits grow
From a single hare. Mutation's friend,
Who could have prophesied the end
When the Spider Woman deftly snared the fly
And the monsters strangled in a monstrous kiss
And somebody hissed, "You'll hang for this!"?

Dear Dracula, sleeping on your native soil,
(Any other kind makes him spoil),
How we clapped when you broke the French door down
And surprised the bride in the overwrought bed.

Perfectly dressed for lunar research,
Your evening cape added much,
Though the bride, inexplicably dressed in furs,
Was a study in jaded jugulars.

Poor, tortured Leopard Man, you changed your spots
In the debauched village of the Pin-Head Tots;
How we wrung our hands, how we wept
When the eighteenth murder proved inept,
And, caught in the Phosphorous Cave of Sea,
Dangling the last of synthetic flesh,
You said, "There's something wrong with me."

The Wolf Man knew when he prowled at dawn
Beginnings spin a web where endings spawn.
The bat who lived on shaving cream,
A household pet of Dr. Dream,
Unfortunately, maddened by the bedlam,
Turned on the Doc, bit the hand that fed him.

And you, Dr. X, who killed by moonlight,
We loved your scream in the laboratory
When the panel slid and the night was starry
And you threw the inventor in the crocodile pit
(An obscure point: Did he deserve it?)
And you took the gold to Transylvania
Where no one guessed how insane you were.

We thank you for the moral and the mood,
Dear Dr. Cliche, Nurse Platitude.
When we meet again by the Overturned Grave,
Near the Sunken City of the Twisted Mind,
(In *The Son of the Son of Frankenstein*),
Make the blood flow, make the motive muddy:
There's a little death in every body.

And here is Langston Hughes, writing in the middle of the Depression about black folks watching white folks' films in the movie palaces of Harlem:

MOVIES

The Roosevelt, Renaissance, Gem, Alhambra:
Harlem laughing in all the wrong places
    at the crocodile tears
    of crocodile art
    that you know
    in your heart
    is crocodile:

    (Hollywood
    laughs at me,
    black—
    so I laugh
    back.)

Both of these poems are to be found in an unexpectedly amusing anthology, *Lights, Camera, Poetry! American Movie Poems: The First Hundred Years,* edited by Jason Shinder and published by Harcourt Brace.

---

Returning to the South is a recurrent theme in African-American songs and poems—from the minstrel composer James Bland's "Carry Me Back to Old Virginny," written in the years after the Civil War, to Fats Waller's brilliant, bitter "Cinders," to the young poet Anthony Walton's recent prose book, interspersed with poems, *Mississippi.* Lucille Clifton, a much-loved American poet, gives us another version in her latest book, *The Terrible Stories* (BOA Editions Ltd.). It comes from a section of the book called "A Term in Memphis":

ENTERING THE SOUTH

i have put on my mother's coat.
it is warm and familiar
as old fur
and i can hear hushed voices
through it.   too many
animals have died
to make this.   the sleeves
coil down to my hands
like rope.   i will wear it
because she loved it
but the blood from it pools
on my shoulders
heavy and dark and alive.

Something haunting to me about the metaphor of the fur coat, and odd. Not just that it makes a kind of parallel between the opening of the West through the fur trade and the cultivation of the South through slavery, but something about the cruel glamour of fur gives the poem, and Clifton's reading of African-American identity, such ambiguity and depth.

In the book this is complicated further by a series of poems in which Clifton makes the fox (and fox fur) a muse figure, a symbol of her own hunger:

FOX

who
can blame her for hunkering
into the doorwells at night,
the only blaze in the dark
the brush of her hopeful tail,
the only starlight
her little bared teeth?

and when she is not satisfied
who can blame her for refusing to leave,
for raising the one paw up and barking,
Master of the Hunt, why am i
not feeding, not being fed.

---

A beloved teacher of poetry, Ernest Sandeen, died recently in South Bend, Ind. He taught generations of students at the University of Notre Dame for the last 40 years. He was always quite modest about his own poems, but he had many admirers, among them the Poet Laureate Robert Pinsky, who described his work this way: "emotion, clarity, seriousness of purpose, formal grace, the imprint of a distinctive mind." In one of his last books, *A Later Day, Another Year,* he wrote about an old poet still visited by the impulse of poetry. Or maybe the poem is modeled on those traditional dialogues in the old poets between the body and the soul:

DIALOGUE AT THE DOOR

I had no intention
of coming this way again,
but here I am. Do you
still have light for me?

Yes, but not as bright as before.

And the darkness?

Not as deep and dense.
Expect sleep to be
foreshortened, dreams more shallow.

Has this place become
more narrow, then, than it was?

No; in fact, much wider,
but air is thinner.
Muscles of mind and body
have to breathe harder.

Well, then, shall I come back in,
as if beginning once more?

Dear old friend, it's not
your choice. You must.

---

I came across a line I liked the other day:

I don't find you behind any eyes you open.

It's from *State of Mind,* a book by Los Angeles poet Martha Ronk, published by Sun & Moon Press. The impulse of a lot of contemporary experimental poetry, of the postmodernists, is to abrade language, to roughen it, to make you look twice rather than to look through it as if it were clear glass. It demands reading, and reminds me of what Toni Morrison is reported to have said when Oprah Winfrey asked her what she'd tell readers who complained that they had to go over her sentences three or four times. Morrison said: "I'd tell them it's called reading, honey."

Here are a couple of poems by Martha Ronk for you to read. The first one seems to be about one of those dry canyons that define the Southern California landscape:

ARROYO SECO

The gap in logic cuts a dry riverbed across the land
unerring in inference and what follows from what isn't there

eroded about the edges of metaphor
where redwood and imported palm catch a glimpse
of the new world. So much remains unseen
despite the broad view or the absence of foliage
rolling down to the arroyo which from a certain vantage
appears swallowed up by point of view.
Drawn to it as drawn to the pointlessness of it all
after a while I couldn't tell if nostalgia was
for a place or a time or before learning to think.

The next one is about what so many song writers have written about.

### THE MOON OVER L.A.

The moon moreover spills onto
the paving stone once under foot.
Plants it there one in front.
She is not more than any other except her shoulders forever.
Keep riding she says vacant as the face of.
Pull over and give us a kiss.
When it hangs over the interchange
she and she and she. A monument to going nowhere,
a piece of work unmade by man. O moon,
rise up and give us ourselves awash and weary—
we've seen it all and don't mind.

I like that funny "moreover," which seems to address the thousands of
things that have already been said about the moon, and jumps into the
conversation. And I like the way that the only metaphor for the moon is
the moon. That seems to be what happens in the fifth line. "vacant as the
face of," she writes, and then, seeing that she was about to say that the face
of the moon was as blank as the face of the moon, she stops, lets the silence
do its work. Interesting writing.

Readers might enjoy puzzling over the fourth line. The moon (or
some woman) is not more except her shoulders? Is this some pun on
things being "head and shoulders" above other things? A sort of send-

up of the classic poetry of mooniness like the 16th-century courtier Sir Philip Sidney's

> With how sad steps, O moon, thou climb'st the skies!
> How silently, and with how wan a face!

If you put this version of the high and the ideal next to Ronk's

> She is no more than any other except her shoulders forever.

you will have your fractured, postmodern Renaissance summer moon for this week. And it seems right for Southern California. You can almost imagine one of Raymond Chandler's tough guy detectives going his lonely way under those shoulders.

---

Here's a mysterious poem from a very rich and illuminating new anthology that covers the entire sweep of Latin American poetry in the 20th century. It's by the Argentine poet Roberto Juarroz and translated by W.S. Merwin:

LIFE DRAWS A TREE

Life draws a tree
and death draws another one.
Life draws a nest
and death copies it.
Life draws a bird
to live in the nest
and right away death
draws another bird.
A hand that draws nothing
wanders among the drawings
and at times moves one of them.

For example
a bird of life
occupies the death's nest
on the tree that life drew.

Other times
the hand that draws nothing
blots out one drawing of the series.
For example
the tree of death
holds the nest of death
but there's no bird in it.

And other times
the hand that draws nothing
itself changes
into an extra image
in the shape of a bird,
in the shape of a tree,
in the shape of a nest.
And then, only then,
nothing's missing and nothing's left over.
For example
two birds
occupy life's nest
in death's tree.

Or life's tree
holds two nests
with only one bird in them.

Or a single bird
lives in one nest
on the tree of life

and the tree of death.

The book is *Twentieth Century Latin American Poetry: A Bilingual Anthology*, edited by Stephen Tapscott and published by University of Texas Press. For everyone who thinks only of Pablo Neruda when they think of Latin American poetry, or of Neruda and Cesar Vallejo and Octavio Paz, this book will be a revelation.

Roberto Juarroz was born in 1925 and died in 1995. He headed the Department of Information Science (as they now call schools for library training) at the University of Buenos Aires. The question about this poem, of course, is what we suppose he meant by or what meaning we give to "a hand that draws nothing" (*uno mano que no dibuja nada*). Something to think about in the dusk as summer deepens into August.

---

I keep reading in the University of Texas Press's *Twentieth Century Latin American Poetry*, edited by Stephen Tapscott. The selection of work by the Brazilian poet Adelia Prado sent me to a fuller collection of her work, *The Alphabet in the Park: Selected Poems of Adelia Prado*, published by Wesleyan University Press and translated by Ellen Watson.

Adelia Prado came to the attention of readers when the great Brazilian poet Carlos Drummond de Andrade announced to newspaper readers that St. Francis was dictating poems to a woman in the state of Minas Gerais, "a landlocked state," her translator says, "of rugged mountains, mines, and baroque churches." She's lived in a small town there most of her life, teaching philosophy and religion and raising a family. She seems to be a kind of Brazilian Catholic Emily Dickinson, but of the 20th century. She's a quirky writer, a passionate and complex thinker, a passionate person. Here's an instance:

DYSRHYTHMIA

Old people spit with absolutely no finesse
and bicycles bully traffic on the sidewalk.
The unknown poet waits for criticism

and reads his verses three times a day
like a monk with his book of hours.
The brush got old and no longer brushes.
Right now what's important
is to untangle the hair.
We give birth between our legs
and go on talking about it til the end,
few of us understanding:
it's the soul that's erotic.
If I want, I put on a Bach aria
so I can feel forgiving and calm.
What I understand of God is His wrath;
there's no other way to say it.
The ball thumping against the wall annoys me,
but the kids laugh, contented.
I've seen hundreds of afternoons like today.
No agony, just an anxious impatience:
something is going to happen.
Destiny doesn't exist.
It's God we need, and fast.

I don't completely get this poem. It proceeds as a series of unconnec-
ted statements. What does the unfastidious spitting of old people have to
do with the unpublished poet or with hair tangled in a disused brush?
And I certainly resist the God of wrath. But there is something about
the way the poem gathers force and the way some statements leap out—
"it's the soul that's erotic," "Destiny doesn't exist"—that is mysterious,
persuasive and a little scary to me. I have felt all week, reading her, in the
presence of a sometimes funny, earthy, but disturbing and urgent spirit.
    Here's one more poem:

DAY

The chickens open their beaks in alarm
and stop, with that knack they have,

immobile—I was going to say immoral—
wattles and coxcombs stark red,
only the arteries quivering in their necks.
A woman startled by sex,
but delighted.

---

Here's a poem for the end of summer from a New Hampshire poet named Alice B. Fogel. It's from her second book, *I Love This Dark World,* published by Zoland Books in Cambridge, Mass. It's a poem that twines the theme of sunflowers around a parent's instinctive fear for her children, and it's written in a complicated, mesmerising, repetitive form, almost sleepy, that seems just right for its theme:

THE SUNFLOWERS

So sated, with sunlight, summertime, and seeds,
the sunflowers bow down their heads.
Made of only bone and soul, I am a darker thing.

While my foolish tears have nothing to breed,
*those* seeds are boats that sail back from the dead
to be sated again with sunlight, summertime, and seed.

I can't forget the babies who could not breathe,
that what might keep them alive was neither love nor dread,
that, made only of bone and soul, I am a dark, dark thing.

Don't tell me about sunflowers, redemption, faith, or need,
about the balance of day and night or of darkness wed
to the sated, to sunlight, to summertime, or seed.

I have seen the cruel gleam of this world's teeth
in my children's darkened rooms. Listen, I said,
they are only made of bone and soul; I am a darker thing.

Fear sobs in my head when I'm too far from them to see—
as if the cord had bled, as if they were already dead
and sated, with sunlight, summertime, and seed,
bone, and soul, and the darkness in everything.

# FALL

Labor Day. After Walt Whitman, the poet who best loved the rhythms of work, the art and energy and precision of the American trades, was William Carlos Williams. Williams was an innovator, trying to figure out how to make poems in the new medium of free verse. What stanza patterns to use without rhyme to justify them, how to make the order of presentation, perception by perception, move with or against the unit of the line. He was interested in craftsmanship, so whenever he wrote about work, he was also writing about the craft of poetry. Here's a poem about the roofing trade; it was first published in 1936, and can be found in the first volume of *The Collected Poems of William Carlos Williams* (it's a two-volume set), published by New Directions and edited by A. Walton Litz and Christopher MacGowan:

### FINE WORK WITH PITCH AND COPPER

Now they are resting
in the fleckless light
separately in unison

like the sacks
of sifted stone stacked
regularly by twos

about the flat roof
ready after lunch
to be opened and strewn

The copper in eight
foot strips has been
beaten lengthwise

down the center at right
angles and lies ready
to edge the coping

One still chewing
picks up a copper strip
and runs his eye along it.

That's it. It's a very American poem. Because of the light, it could be a Thomas Eakins painting, and it's as lean, efficient, and graceful as a stunt in a Buster Keaton two-reeler. It's also about an ideal, caught in the unconscious gesture of the workman thinking about his task and his materials: A whole world rises from it of made things constructed by people who work hard and can't help thinking about their craft.

---

I spent some time in August in the west of Scotland, on the Isle of Skye in the Inner Hebrides, and in the west of Ireland, in Galway and the Aran Islands. And I haunted bookstores afterwards in Dublin because the whole experience made me hungry for the language of those places. On the long flight home I read the poems of George Mackay Brown, a Scottish poet of the remote Orkney Islands in the far north, who died last year. His *Selected Poems: 1954–1992* was published in the United States by the University of Iowa Press, and it was just what I wanted. Brown was born in Stromness in the Orkneys in 1921 and lived for 70 years, with a few out for schooling in Edinburgh, on those islands.

The whole body of his work is richer than I can convey with one poem. But for me his language catches exactly the harrowing beauty of those stony islands, and his poems are rich in their history and lore. Seamus Heaney, who must clearly have felt his influence in his own early poems, describes his style as having "something of the skaldic poet's consciousness of inevitable ordeal, something of the haiku master's susceptibility to the delicate and momentary." It seems an odd combination but it's accurate. The short poems, which Brown calls "runes," he writes as sequences. Here's one from "Runes from the Island of Horses":

WINTER

Three winter brightnesses—
Bridesheet, boy in snow,
Kirkyard spade.

That gravedigger's spade, almost white from use, is what must have put Heaney in mind of the haiku poet's eye. But the rhythms—*bridesheet, kirkyard*—have the surge of old Anglo-Saxon verse. And Brown uses it to imagine and render the whole history of those islands—neolithic stone circles, Norse raiders and settlers, Scottish smugglers and farmers and fishermen, the coming of Christianity from Ireland, the struggle between the Church of Rome and the Calvinism of Geneva, the ages-long conflict between the crofters, peasant farmers, and the lairds, the landlord class—all set among those seaside sheep pastures and barley fields and windswept skerries.

Here's a typical poem, if there is one, or at least an archetypal one. You still see men in the fields digging peat from the bogs in both Scotland and Ireland and stacked bricks of it, looking like some form of matter halfway between mud and coal, drying on the roadsides:

PEAT CUTTING

And we left our beds in the dark
And we drove a cart to the hill
And we buried the jar of ale in the bog
And our small blades glittered in the dayspring
And we tore dark squares, thick pages
From the Book of Fire
And we spread them wet on the heather
And horseflies, poisonous hooks,
Stuck in our arms
And we laid off our coats
And our blades sank deep into water
And the lord of the bog, the kestrel
Paced round the sun

And at noon we leaned on our tuskars
—The cold unburied jar
Touched, like a girl, a circle of burning mouths
And the boy found a wild bees' comb
And his mouth was a sudden brightness
And the kestrel fell
And a lark flashed a needle across the west
And we spread a thousand peats
Between one summer star
And the black chaos of fire at the earth's centre.

A tuskar, according to my dictionary, is "an implement for cutting peats used in Orkney and Shetland," so the word could hardly be more local or more literal. It comes from the Old Norse *torf* (turf) plus *skera* (to shear). So a *torfsker* in Norse became a *tuskar* in Gaelic, and then in English.

---

I'm going to continue to inflict my summer adventures on my patient readers.

From the Isle of Skye in mid-August we drove south through the highlands to Glasgow, stopping at Loch Lomand on a green, drizzly afternoon to croon out, more or less on key, "Loch Lomand" to the echoing glens in homage to Robert Burns. From Glasgow we flew to Galway to attend the Aran Islands Poetry Festival. One of the readings was held on the island of Inishmore, in a 2000-year-old fort, Dun Eochlan: slabs of black limestone, the stony body of the island, set without mortar and with such skill they were still standing on a hill above the sea these two millennia later. A poet of the island, an old man, recited in Irish his own poems and some poems of the old Celtic-language poet known as Blind Raftery and other poems from the oral tradition that went back centuries. It was like hearing the tail end of the tradition of oral recitation from which Homer emerged.

Another reader was Mary O'Malley, a Galway poet, a woman in her late thirties or early forties, mother of two children, who took the ferry from Galway once a week and taught a poetry workshop for the islanders. Here's a poem she read about the life of the place:

### A YOUNG MATRON DANCES FREE OF THE ISLAND

One Tuesday in November she finished the wash-up,
Mounted a white horse
And rode into the force nine waves
Out beyond the lighthouse.
Feck it, she said, startling the neighbors,
It's go now or be stuck here forever
Chained to this rock like that Greek,
With the gannets tearing at my liver.

She rode bareback out the roads. The horse reared
But climbed the foothills of the breakers.
When she heard her children calling
Mama, mama, she turned, praying
Jesus, let me make shore
And I will never desert them again,
Nor be ungrateful. When she got in
Half drowned, there was no-one there.

For weeks in the psychiatric all she could see
Were graveyards, men laid out in coffins,
The little satin curtains
They would have shunned in life, of palest ivory
About to be drawn. It was the long winters
They say, drove her out again
To where there was no going back.
She loved parties, was a beautiful dancer—

There is no other explanation.
The husband was good to her, by all accounts.
Does it matter? There should be a moment,
A shard of glass to hold against the light,
A checkpoint to pass before the end.
He has nothing, though people are kind.
They say her hair caught the sun
As she waltzed over the cliff, haloing beautifully down.

---

In Dublin—this will be my last report from the field—in August, after we left the Aran Islands, we saw what turned out to be a very stagey and melodramatic production of Sean O'Casey's "Juno and the Paycock" at the Abbey Theater. The interesting thing about it was that the play itself seemed to me much better than I remembered. What I recalled was the banter between the Captain and his drinking buddy Joxer—"Ah, it's a darlin' moon, Captain, a darlin' moon"—and the politics. "Haven't I done enough for Ireland?" the maimed young man pleads to his superior in the IRA, and the IRA functionary, in his trenchcoat, says, "No man has done enough for Ireland." The Abbey played it for these big scenes, but underneath the stage fire is a much shrewder and more subtle study of the family: the helpless vortex of blustering and impotent father and long-suffering mother, the son torn between his anger and a sort of crushed piety, the daughter between her sexuality and her longing for gentility. It seemed to me that the less the play was about the drama of Irishness, the more its real power would become apparent.

And that made me realize that I was reading Irish poetry in the same way: looking for the poetry of place names and landscapes and the history and drama of Irish politics. Understandable, of course, but it's the same reason why the postcards show us old guys in tweed caps outside of pubs and not men and women in suits driving their Datsuns to work through the Dublin traffic.

My host in Dublin was Dennis O'Driscoll, a poet who left a farming family in Tipperary at the age of 16, went to Dublin, and got a job as a clerk in a government office. He's worked in the Civil Service ever since, written four books of poems and become one of the best-known reviewers and commentators on Irish poetry. In his newest book, *Quality Time* (Anvil Press, London), he writes in a dry, ironic way—something of W.H. Auden and something of Philip Larkin in the style—about office life. It's the antithesis of the intensely poetic subject matter Americans associate with Irish poetry. And it's close to home, maybe too close—the language makes almost no effort to rise up out of its material. Here are three sections from the title poem:

### THE BOTTOM LINE

Official standards, building regulations,
fair procedures for dismissing errant staff:
my brain is crammed with transient knowledge
—patent numbers, EC directives, laws.
I pause at traffic lights on the way back
to headquarters; windscreen wipers skim off
visions of this seeping stone-faced town:
a warehouse frontage littered with crates,
lovers locked in an umbrella-domed embrace,
consumers at a bank dispenser drawing cash.
I race the engine, inch the car toward green.

&

Quality time at weekends, domestic bliss:
early pathways cordoned off by webs,
I slip out to the shops, return
to bring you tea and newspapers in bed.
On Sundays, every Sunday, I submit to the calm
of supplements, CDs, cooking smells.
All of the mornings of all of the weekdays
I leave for work; my office bin fills
with the shredded waste of hours.
A pattern regular as wallpaper or rugs
and no more permanent than their flowers.

The peace of Friday evenings after
staff have left the open‑plan deserted,
before cleaners key‑in for their shift.
Sun flakes out on the carpets, rays
highlight staplers, calculators, pens;
phones flop in cradles: Monday will
inaugurate another week, small talk
over instant coffee, new debenture stock ...
Meanwhile, suspended between worlds, I drum
on the plastic in‑tray, stare down at
the frenzied city, disinclined to budge.

Ten‑syllable lines, sometimes stretched to 12, roughly iambic. Shakespeare's meter at the end of the 20th century: "Consumers at a bank dispenser drawing cash."

---

I've begun to read in the new books of poems that appear in the fall like an apple harvest. The most talked‑about of them is Jorie Graham's *The Errancy* (Ecco Press). Graham re‑ceived the Pulitzer Prize for her selected poems, *The Dream of the Unified Field* (also Ecco), last year, and this book, her first new collection in some time, is one of her best. It arrives just after a relentlessly urbane *New Yorker* profile of her, which, as *New Yorker* profiles tend to, gave us a por‑trait of the poet and her endearing quirks and has almost nothing to say about the urgency and vision of the poems.

People always say about Graham that her poems are big and ambi‑tious, that she's a gorgeous writer, and she's notoriously "difficult," as a lot of original poets are. Her difficulty usually has to do with her magic, and part of her magic comes from the fact that her poems are not always easy to locate. For example, the last poem in her new book describes a man in robes dancing down an alley at sundown. Who or what is he? The poem doesn't tell us. He could be a man dancing down an alley, a Chaplinesque or harlequinesque figure perhaps, seen or imagined. Or he could be a metaphor for the dancing of the wind. Or for poetry. Or for a certain freedom that only the human soul sometimes has. There is even a moment when you think it may be a figure conjured while listening to music.

Graham is also notoriously intelligent, and the intelligence of the poems often consists in leaps of imagination, or leaps of inference. And, in the way of intelligence, these leaps can feel like sudden, surprising turns. They're not what you expected and they need to be read and read again. For example, the last eight lines of this same poem:

### OF THE EVER-CHANGING AGITATION IN THE AIR

The man held his hands to his heart as he danced.
He slacked and swirled.
The doorways of the little city
blurred. Something
leaked out,
kindling the doorframes up,
making each entranceway
less true.
And darkness gathered
*although it does not fall.* . . . And the little dance,
swinging this human all down the alleyway,
nervous little theme pushing itself along,
braiding, rehearsing,
constantly incomplete so turning and tacking—
oh what is there to finish?—his robes made rustic by the reddish
    swirl,
which grows darker towards the end of the avenue of course,
one hand on his chest,
one flung out to the side as he dances, taps, sings,
on his scuttling toes, now humming a little,
now closing his eyes as he twirls, growing smaller,

why does the sun rise? remember me always dear for I will
return—
*liberty* spooring in the evening air,
into which the lilacs open, the skirts uplift,
liberty and the blood-eye careening gently over the giant earth,
and the cat in the doorway who does not mistake the world,
eyeing the spots where the birds must eventually land—

---

Derek Walcott was born on the island of Santa Lucia in
1930 and won the Nobel Prize for Literature in 1992.
It's always been hard to know how to describe him.
Afro-Caribbean, the musical term, doesn't seem right. Part African,
part—I think—Irish, a black man according to the tribal politics of the
western hemisphere, he was educated in the English colonial tradition;
his head and his poems are full of the rhythms of English poetry. He had
to find his own way to make an American poetry, and he was not drawn,
at least not directly, to the black poetics of French Caribbean poets like
the Haitian Aimee Cesaire. Of the same generation as Allen Ginsberg
and Frank O'Hara, his poetry seems classical in comparison. His task
was to make a Caribbean poetry: an American poetry of the tropics, a
region which might include in its literature, if you reimagine the map in
your mind, William Faulkner and Gabriel Garcia Marquez.

His new book, *The Bounty* (Farrar, Straus & Giroux), includes an
elegy for his mother and a series of intensely imagined poems about his
home place. Nostalgia is a tricky matter in poetry, in life. If it does not
have an almost visionary intensity, the feeling can seem too easy. Here he
holds it up to death and seems to locate his writing in the place between
death and the intense presence of his native place. The poem is untitled.

Never get used to this; the feathery, swaying casuarinas,
the morning silent light on shafts of bright grass,
the growing *Aves* of the ocean, the white lances of the marinas,
the surf fingering its beads, hail heron and gull full of grace,

since that is all you need to do now at your age
and its coming serene extinction like the light on the shale
at sunset, and your gift fading out of this page;
your soul travelled the one horizon, like a quiet snail,
infinity behind it, infinity ahead of it,
and all that it knew was this craft, all that it wanted—
what did it know of death? Only what you had read of it,
that it was like a flame blown out in a lowered lantern,
a night, but without these stars, the prickle of planets, lights
like a vast harbour, or devouring oblivion;
never get used to this, the great moon on these studded nights
that make the heart stagger; and the stirring lion
of the headland. This is why you have ended, to pass,
praising the feathery swaying of the casuarinas
and those shudderings of thanks, that so often descended,
the evening light in the shafts of feathery grass,
the lances fading, then the lights of the marinas,
the yachts studying their reflection in black glass.

---

A poem for the harvest season, from Carol Muske's *An Octave Above Thunder: New and Selected Poems* (Penguin). A critic and novelist as well as a poet, Muske has just published a collection of essays, *Women and Poetry: Autobiography and the Shape of Truth*.

THE INVENTION OF CUISINE

Imagine for a moment
the still life of our meals,
meat followed by yellow cheese,
grapes pale against the blue armor of fish.

Imagine a thin woman
before bread was invented,

playing a harp of wheat in the field.
There is a stone, and behind her
the bones of the last killed,
the black bird on her shoulder
that a century later
will fly with murderous and trained intent.

They are not very hungry
because cuisine has not yet been invented.
Nor has falconry,
nor the science of imagination.

All they have is the pure impulse to eat,
which is not enough to keep them alive
and this little moment
before the woman redeems
the sprouted seeds at her feet
and gathers the olives falling from the trees
for her recipes.

Imagine. Out in the fields
this very moment
they are rolling the apples to press,
the lamb turns in a regular aura of smoke.

See, the woman looks behind her
before picking up the stone,
looks back once at the beasts,
the trees,
that sky
above the white stream
where small creatures live and die
looking upon each other
as food.

"So we traveled with a mote in each eye," a poem by Michael Palmer goes, "always parallel to the horizon, always sideways Clouds rose from crumbling brick where symmetries spoke of bread They spoke of letters lost in cellars and halls and whispered the coming of snow though far too softly to be heard." Palmer is a philosophical poet—or the poet of this generation most at home in the wilderness made by 20th-century philosophy, which has addressed itself mostly to what we don't know, can't know, can't say. The world, Wittgenstein observed, is all that is the case, and language, Derrida observed, displaces the world. Truth, Wittgenstein remarked, means that all ravens are black until you see a white raven. The problem of how one writes in a world stripped bare by philosophy and harrowed by a century of unspeakable violence is the subject of many of Palmer's poems. Here is one from his newest book, *At Passages* (New Directions):

AUTOBIOGRAPHY

All clocks are clouds.
Parts are greater than the whole.
A philosopher is starving in a rooming house, while it rains
  outside.
He regards the self as just another sign.
Winter roses are invisible.
Late ice sometimes sings.

*A* and *Not-A* are the same.
My dog does not know me.
Violins, like dreams, are suspect.
I come from Kolophon, or perhaps some small island.
The strait was frozen, and people are walking—a few skating—
  across it.
On the crescent beach, a drowned deer.

A woman with one hand, her thighs around your neck.
The world is all that is displaced.

Apples in a stall sat the streetcorner by the Bahnhof, pale yellow
    to blackish red.
Memory does not speak.
Shortness of breath, accompanied by tinnitus.

The poet's stutter and the philosopher's.
The self is assigned to others.
A room from which, at all times, the moon remains visible.
Leningrad cafe: a man missing the left side of his face.
Disappearance of the sun from the sky above Odessa.
True description of that sun.
A philosopher lies in a doorway, discussing the theory of colors

with himself
the theory of self with himself, the concept of number, eternal
    return, the sidereal pulse
logic of types, Buridan sentences, the *lekton*.
Why now that smoke off the lake?
Word and thing are the same.
Many times white ravens have I seen.

That all planes are infinite, by extension.
She asks, Is there a map of these gates?
She asks, Is this the one called Passages, or is it that one to the
    west?
Thus released, the dark angels converse with the angels of light.
They are not angels.
Something else.

Jane Hirshfield has become familiar to readers for her translation of two women poets of the 8th-century Japanese court who were among the creators of the Japanese lyric poem. The book is called *The Ink Dark Moon,* and it's well worth looking for. Hirshfield also edited an anthology of spiritual poetry by women from all over the world and from every century, *Women in Praise of the Sacred.* Hirshfield's religious interests come from her training in Zen Buddhism. A native of New Jersey, educated at Princeton, she lives in northern California. Her newest book of poems, *Lives of the Heart,* was just published by HarperCollins. Here's a sample:

KNOWING NOTHING

Love is not the reason.
Love is the lure,
the thin goat staked out in the clearing.

The lion has stalked
the village for a long time.
It does not want the goat,
who stands thin and bleating,
tied to its bit of wood.

The goat is not the reason.
The reason is the lion,
whose one desire is to enter—
Not the goat, which is
only the lure, only excuse,
but the one burning life
it has hunted for a long time
disguised as hunger. Disguised as love.
Which is not the reason.

Or would you think
that the bones of a lion reason?
Would you think that the tongue?

The lion does not want the goat,
It only wants to live. Alone if it must.
In pain if it must. Knowing nothing.
Like the goat, it only wants to live.
Like love. Or would you think that the heart?

---

After Halloween. I was raised a Catholic and the nuns, when I was in school, always emphasized that the holiday was the eve of All Souls' Day. So that we did not think it was only about bagging candy and wearing costumes. It did not make me more Christian, the idea of the spirits of the undead wandering the earth, and I always think of it at this time of year, having also read about the rituals humans have devised to allay or ward off the restless ghosts they live among.

Here's a poem, a rather sweet poem, by the New York poet Thomas Lux. Lux is a poet of—usually—bitter wit, of the kind of irony that comes with a quick, impatient intelligence. He can also be darkly funny. I've been reading his *New and Selected Poems, 1975–95* (Houghton Mifflin), a book full of sanity and dismay. A poem called "Money" begins: "It's a paper product." A poem called "The People of the Other Village" begins "hate the people of this village" and turns out to be a history of the world: "We do this, they do that. Ten thousand years." But, today, this other poem caught my eye, about a live child in this season and the restless ghost of a marriage:

CRISS CROSS APPLE SAUCE

*Criss cross apple sauce*
*do me a favor and get lost*
*while you're at it drop dead*
*then come back without a head*
my daughter sings for me
when I ask her what she learned in school today

as we drive from her mother's house to mine.
She knows I like some things that rhyme.
She sings another she knows I like:
*Trick or treat, trick or treat*
*give me something good to eat*
*If you don't I don't care*
*I'll put apples in your underwear...*
Apples in your underwear—I like that more
than Lautreamont's umbrella
on the operating table, I say to her
and ask if she sees the parallel.
She says no but she prefers the apples too.
*Sitting on a bench*
*nothing to do*
*along come some boys—p.u., p.u., p.u.*
my daughter sings,
my daughter with her buffalo-size heart,
my daughter brilliant and kind,
my daughter singing
as we drive from her mother's house to mine.

Lautreamont was a French poet, one of the precursors of surrealism.
I don't know the story about the umbrella. One of these days I'll look it
up. For now it's a ghost of meaning hovering around the poem.

---

John Balaban, some twenty years ago, wrote one of the best
books of poems about Vietnam by an American, *After Our
War*. Since then, he's translated Vietnamese folk poetry. In
*Locusts at the Edge of Summer: New and Selected Poems* (Copper Canyon),
there are several newer poems that revisit those days:

The French ships shelled Haiphong then took the port.
Mr. Giai was running down a road, mobilized
with two friends, looking for their unit in towns
where thatch and geese lay shattered on the roads
and smoke looped up from cratered yards. A swarm
of bullock carts and bicycles streamed against them
as trousered women strained with children, chickens,
charcoal, and rice towards Hanoi in the barrage lull.
Then, Giai said, they saw just stragglers.
Ahead, the horizon thumped with bombs.

At an empty inn they tried their luck
though the waiter said he'd nothing left.
"Just a coffee," said Mr. Giai. "A sip
of whiskey," said one friend. "A cigarette," the other.
Miraculously, these each appeared. Serene,
they sat a while, then went to fight.
Giai wrote a poem about that pause in *Ve Quoc Quan,*
the Army paper. Critics found the piece bourgeois.

Forty years of combat now behind him
—Japanese, Americans, and French.
Wounded twice, deployed in jungles for nine years,
his son just killed in Cambodia,
Giai tells this tale to three Americans
each young enough to be his son:
an ex-Marine once rocketed in Hue,
an Army grunt, mortared at Bong Son,
a c.o. hit by a stray of shrapnel,

all four silent in the floating restaurant
rocking on moor-lines in the Saigon river.
Crabshells and beer bottles litter their table.
A rat runs a rafter overhead. A wave slaps by.

"That moment," Giai adds, "was a little like now."
They raise their glasses to the river's amber light,
all four as quiet as if carved in ivory.

---

The best known of all autumn haiku is by Bashō and like most of his poems, it's very simple:

> A crow
> just settled on a bare branch—
> autumn evening

This one is not so simple—

> What voice,
> what song, spider,
> in the autumn wind

—because spiders are silent. Sometimes he notices the vegetables of the season. This poem, written while he was travelling, has a title, or head-note:

AT A HERMITAGE:

> A cool fall night—
> getting dinner, we peeled
> eggplants, cucumbers.

The fall in Japanese poetry is often associated with partings, and with loneliness. This is a departure poem:

> Autumn ending,
> and we part,
> clamshells on the beach.

The hinged, empty clamshells are actually there, but they are also a metaphor for the feeling of connection and loss. And the poem he wrote just before he died is a poem of the late fall:

> Sick on a journey,
> my dreams wander
> the withered fields.

These translations come from *The Essential Haiku,* but if you want to study the form, there are a number of books available. Best, if you can find them, are the four volumes of R.H. Blythe's *Haiku,* published by Hokuseido Press in Tokyo.

---

For Thanksgiving a poem about the holiday by a poet who sees it with European eyes. Laure-Anne Bosselaar was born in Flemish Belgium and has published poems in French. *The Hour Between Dog and Wolf* (Boa Editions) is her first book in English.

### INVENTORY

Thanksgiving today. Soaked with sleet.
No sun for six days—six is the Devil's number.
I have looked through this window,
at these American skies for two times six years.
My wall is covered with photographs of distant friends.

This is my third garden. The first two blossomed in Belgium.
Where there is no Thanksgiving. Where my father is buried.
Where I was raised and raped and worked. Where I had five lovers,
but loved only one. Where I gave birth to three children.
A blond son, a dead daughter, a blond daughter.

Shadows grew in my first garden. Two larches in my second.
Because of North sea winds and how they stood, they fused

into one trunk. It wounded them at first, that rubbing together—
the frailest larch loosing sap for months, a lucid sap that glued them
to each other at last. I saw it as an omen for my life.

I give thanks for the lowlands in Belgium.
For Flanders, her canals and taciturn skies. For the tall ships
on the river Scheldt. For coal pyramids in Wallonia.
For the color of hop, and the hop-pickers' songs.
For Antwerp's whores who woo sailors in six different tongues.

Six is the Devil's number. My grandfather and a farmer
killed six German soldiers and threw them in a Flemish moor.
I can no longer give thanks for that: I ask mercy.
Before I die, I'll plant a larch by the moor—*miserere*—
the soldiers' mothers will never know it was done.

I prayed six times for the death of my Jew-hating father,
I ask mercy for that also: it's Thanksgiving today.
I give thanks for my son and daughter, for the man I love
who taught me a new language.
For this garden's life and sleet.

Before I left for this vast continent,
I stole sand from the river Scheldt,
an inch of barbed wire from a Concentration Camp near Antwerp,
a leaf from the chestnut tree behind Apollinaire's grave,
but no weed, not a seed of it, growing from my father's ashes.

In Belgium, the day is almost over.
Soon, a new century will make History: *miserere.*
Four larches grow in my garden: one for my son, one for my
daughter—
and far from a moor in Flanders, the other two fuse
here: in America. In America.

S eamus Heaney's most recent book is *The Spirit Level* (Farrar, Straus & Giroux). I printed one of his poems, I think, just two years ago in the first *Poet's Choice* column, after the announcement that he had received the Nobel Prize. This is his first book since then. In his Nobel lecture he spoke of a poetry that could "persuade the vulnerable part of our consciousness of its rightness." Here's the last poem in the new book:

POSTSCRIPT

And some time make the time to drive out west
Into County Clare, along the Flaggy Shore,
In September or October, when the wind
And the light are working off each other
So that the ocean on one side is wild
With foam and glitter, and inland among stones
The surface of a slate-grey lake is lit
By the earthed lightning of a flock of swans.
Their feathers roughed and ruffling, white on white,
Their fully grown headstrong-looking heads
Tucked or cresting or busy underwater.
Useless to think you'll park and capture it
More thoroughly. You are neither here nor there,
A hurry through which known and strange things pass
As big soft buffetings come at the car sideways
And catch the heart off guard and blow it open.

# Sources

ALICE JAMES BOOKS
(affiliate of the University of Maine at Farmington)
a division of Alice James Poetry Cooperative, Inc.
98 Main Street
Farmington, ME 04938

BOA EDITIONS, LTD.
260 East Avenue
Rochester, NY 14604

COPPER CANYON PRESS
P.O. Box 271
Port Townsend, WA 98368

J. M. DENT
an imprint of Orion Publishing
5 Upper St. Martin's Lane
London WC2H 9EA
U.K.

DOUBLEDAY
a division of Bantam Doubleday Dell Publishing Group, Inc.
1540 Broadway
New York, NY 10036

THE ECCO PRESS
100 West Broad Street
Hopewell, NJ 08525

FABER & FABER, LTD.
3 Queen Square
London WC1N 3AU
U.K.

FARRAR, STRAUS & GIROUX, INC.
19 Union Square West
New York, NY 10003

GRAYWOLF PRESS
2402 University Avenue
Suite 203
Saint Paul, MN 55114

HARCOURT BRACE & COMPANY
15 East 26 Street
New York, NY 10010

HARPERCOLLINS PUBLISHERS, INC.
10 East 53rd Street
New York, NY 10022

HENRY HOLT AND COMPANY, INC.
115 West 18th Street
New York, NY 10011

HOUGHTON MIFFLIN COMPANY
222 Berkeley Street
Boston, MA 02116

ALFRED A. KNOPF, INC.
201 East 50th Street
New York, NY 10022

LITTLE, BROWN AND CO., INC.
34 Beacon Street
Boston, MA 02108

LIVERIGHT PUBLISHING CORP.
500 Fifth Avenue
New York, NY 10110

LOUISIANA STATE UNIVERSITY PRESS
P.O. Box 25053
Baton Rouge, LA 70894-5053

MARSILIO PUBLISHERS, INC.
853 Broadway
Suite 600
New York, NY 10003

NEW DIRECTIONS PUBLISHING CORP.
80 Eighth Avenue
New York, NY 10011

W. W. NORTON & CO., INC.
500 Fifth Avenue
New York, NY 10110

OXFORD UNIVERSITY PRESS
198 Madison Avenue
New York, NY 10016

PANTHEON BOOKS
a division of Random House, Inc.
201 East 50th Street
New York, NY 10022

PENGUIN USA
375 Hudson Street
New York, NY 10014

PICADOR
an imprint of St. Martin's Press
175 Fifth Avenue
New York, NY 10010

PRINCETON UNIVERSITY PRESS
41 William Street
Princeton, NJ 08540

RANDOM HOUSE, INC.
201 East 50th Street
New York, NY 10022

SARABANDE BOOKS
2234 Dundee Road
Suite 200
Louisville, KY 40205

SCRIBNER
an imprint of Simon & Schuster
1230 Avenue of the Americas
New York, NY 10020

SIMON & SCHUSTER
1633 Broadway
New York, NY 10019-6785

ST. MARTIN'S PRESS
175 Fifth Avenue
New York, NY 10010

SUN & MOON PRESS
a program of the Contemporary Arts and Education Project, Inc.
6026 Wilshire Boulevard
Los Angeles, CA 90036

TEXAS TECH UNIVERSITY PRESS
P.O. Box 41037
Lubbock, TX 79409

UNIVERSITY OF AKRON PRESS
374/B Bierce Library
Akron, OH 44325/1703

UNIVERSITY OF ARIZONA PRESS
1230 North Park Avenue
Suite 102
Tucson, AZ 85719

UNIVERSITY OF CHICAGO PRESS
5801 Ellis Avenue
Chicago, IL 60637

UNIVERSITY OF NOTRE DAME PRESS
Notre Dame, IN 46556

UNIVERSITY PRESS OF NEW ENGLAND
23 South Main Street
Hanover, NH 03755/2048

VINTAGE BOOKS
a division of Random House, Inc.
201 East 50th Street
New York, NY 10022

WESLEYAN UNIVERSITY PRESS
100 Mount Vernon Street
Middletown, CT 06459/0433

YALE UNIVERSITY PRESS
302 Temple Street
New Haven, CT 06511

ZOLAND BOOKS
384 Huron Avenue
Cambridge, MA 02138

# Copyright Acknowledgments

# Index by Author & Title

# About the Author

Robert Hass served as United States Poet Laureate from 1995 to 1997. He is the author of *Sun Under Wood* (1996), *Human Wishes* (1989), *Praise* (1979), and *Field Guide* (1973). He has co-translated poetry by Czeslaw Milosz and con- tributed to *Dante's Inferno: Translations by Twenty Contemporary Poets*. He has edited *Selected Poems: 1954–1986* by Tomas Tranströmer, as well as *The Essential Haiku: Versions of Bashō, Buson, and Issa*. A book of his essays, *Twentieth Century Pleasures*, which received the National Book Critics Circle Award for criticism in 1984, was recently reissued by Ecco. His many honors include a MacArthur Fellowship. Robert Hass teaches at the University of California at Berkeley.